Fishing Texas

Help Us Keep This Guide Up to Date

Every effort has been made by the author and editors to make this guide as accurate and useful as possible. However, many things can change after a guide is published—roads are detoured, phone numbers change, facilities come under new management, etc.

We would love to hear from you concerning your experiences with this guide and how you feel it could be improved and kept up to date. While we may not be able to respond to all comments and suggestions, we'll take them to heart and we'll also make certain to share them with the author. Please send your comments and suggestions to the following address:

Globe Pequot Press
Reader Response/Editorial Department
PO Box 480
Guilford, CT 06437

Or you may e-mail us at:

editorial@GlobePequot.com

Thanks for your input, and happy fishing!

Fishing
Texas

An Angler's Guide to
the Area's Prime Fishing Spots

BARRY ST.CLAIR

LYONS PRESS
GUILFORD, CONNECTICUT
AN IMPRINT OF GLOBE PEQUOT PRESS

To buy books in quantity for corporate use
or incentives, call **(800) 962-0973**
or e-mail **premiums@GlobePequot.com.**

Lyons Press is an imprint of Globe Pequot Press.

All photos by Barry St.Clair.

Project Editor: Heather Santiago
Layout: Mary Ballachino
Maps by Design Maps Inc. © Morris Book Publishing, LLC

Library of Congress Cataloging-in-Publication Data is available on file.

ISBN 978-1-59921-254-8

Printed in the United States of America
10 9 8 7 6 5 4 3 2 1

Contents

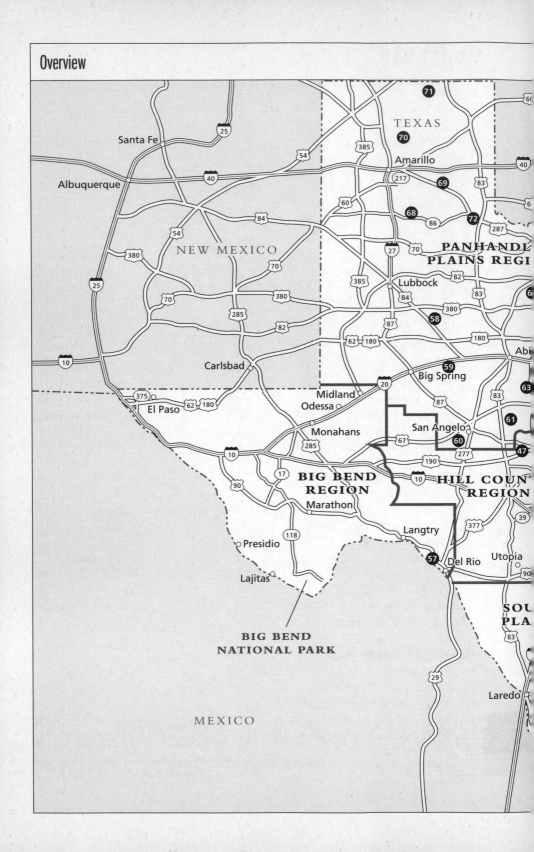

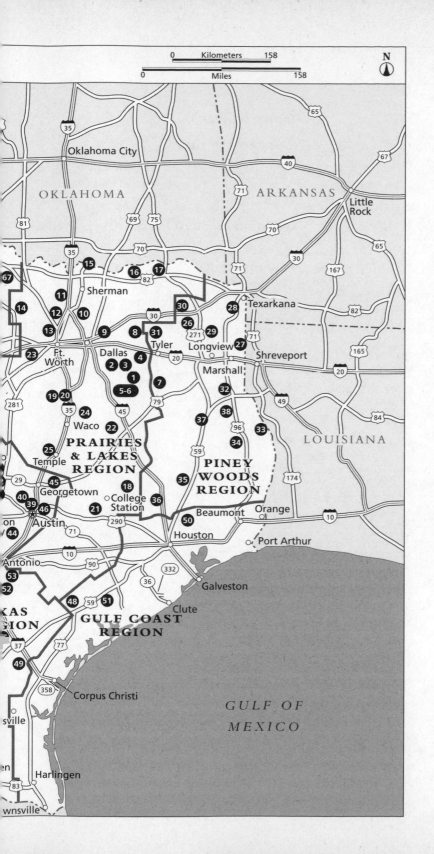

Map Legend

Transportation

≡⟨40⟩≡   Interstate Highway

≡⟨83⟩≡   US Highway

≡⟨86⟩≡   State Highway

≡⟨21⟩≡   Local/County/Forest Road

Water Features

Body of Water

River/Creek

Land Management

National Park/
Forest Boundary

Symbols

✕   Airport

❶   Fishing Site

○   Town

Piney Woods Region

Hill Country Region

Gulf Coast Region

South Texas Plains Region

Big Bend Region

Panhandle Plains Region

Acknowledgments

Writing a book is a complex process. It takes a lot of support from many people to make it happen. I am forever grateful to my parents, John and Edna, for instilling in me an unflagging enthusiasm for all things outdoors. The childhood trips we took as a family are responsible for the outdoor passion I continue to possess. My wife, Gail, is due a large amount of credit for the completion of this project. Her unfailing confidence in my abilities kept me going when momentum or direction ran out. To my son, Wes, I owe a debt of gratitude for his enthusiastic help on detailing the maps. Daughter Lindsey was instrumental in keeping me focused and staying on task. I especially want to thank all the fishing friends and guides who provided information on the various lakes and the best techniques for catching fish from them. I am particularly indebted to many Texas Parks and Wildlife District Fisheries biologists, too numerous to name individually, who contributed greatly to the information presented on each lake featured in their respective districts. Their names are listed in the appendix.

Foreword

What is it about fishing that is so compelling to so many? Based on surveys conducted by the United States Fish and Wildlife Service, millions of Americans fish at least once or twice a year. Anglers spend billions of dollars annually on equipment, services, and fees, and yet catch rates per fishing attempt average below one fish per outing. Does this make any sense?

As I contemplate the answers to the above questions, a north wind is blowing outside my office and the chilling effect of it feels as though the temperature is in the 30s F. Yet, given a choice of working or going fishing on a day such as this, I would choose fishing. Perhaps seventeenth-century writer Thomas D'Urfey said it best:

> Of all the world's enjoyments
> That ever valued were
> There's none of our employments
> With fishing can compare.

Unquestionably, history provides some of the answers. Man was a hunter-gatherer for a long time before the conveniences of agriculture were discovered. Subsistence fishing was a major part of getting us where we are today. And some cultures are still dependent on the practice. So, part of our desire for catching fish is a result of our genetic makeup. We are programmed to be fishermen by the ancient and continuous need for food. Even though that response is now archaic, those of us possessing the fishing gene cannot ignore the call.

Another motivational force is the quest for solace in surroundings that evoke a mind-quieting atmosphere. Modern life is stressful, and from time to time we need a place where the only sounds are those of natural things: winds sighing softly through the leaves; the pleasant hum of bees gathering food from bank-side flowers; the comforting lap of wavelets against the side of a boat. Herbert Hoover said, "Fishing is the chance to wash one's soul with pure air; with the rush of the brook, or with the shimmer of the sun on blue water." Fishing is an all-consuming form of self-psychology. The simple act of casting a lure repeatedly, the focused enjoyment of watching the end of a rod tip for a telltale quiver, or the quiet contemplation of observing a colorful bobber merrily dancing on surface ripples has awesome psychic healing power. The quest for peace and the act of fishing becomes one, and benefits to the mind and soul abound.

Yet, the greatest appeal of this ancient sport born by necessity long ago lies perhaps in the faith of those who embrace it. The act of casting a tidbit tied on the end of a gossamer thread into an alien environment is done in the spirit of anticipation. It is a form of first contact; an attempt to interact with another, lesser species. It is indulgence in wonder, waiting and hoping for a response. Fishing is putting a note in a bottle and casting it into a river or the sea, or tying a message to a balloon and launching it with the wind. These are frivolous feats, but inherently satisfying.

> *The charm of fishing is that it is the pursuit of what is elusive but attainable, a perpetual series of occasions for hope.*
> —John Buchan, nineteenth-century Scottish politician

Introduction

Texas is a huge and diverse landscape that contains at least seven different ecological regions. Each has its own character and geography, which directly affects the kinds and types of fish and fishing available to anglers. Fishing opportunities in Texas abound and can largely be attributed to the severe droughts experienced in the Lone Star State in the early 1950s. Water supplies were found to be inadequate for the state's growing population back then, so Texans went on a reservoir-building frenzy. By 1960 more than 220,000 surface acres of water had been impounded. During the 1960s another 660,000 acres were added. Many different species of fish were stocked into those lakes by public and private agencies. Those new reservoirs formed the backbone of what Texas freshwater fishing has become.

Since then many more impoundments have been added to the total list. Today there are 203 major lakes in Texas, according to Wikipedia, and all of them offer some form of recreational fishing opportunities. Fifteen major river systems feed those reservoirs scattered across the state, and those streams also provide some remarkable fishing. Today Texas has 7,364 square miles of inland waters, according to the *Texas Almanac,* second only to Alaska. That is a remarkable statistic considering that Texas has only one natural reservoir, Caddo Lake, which forms part of the eastern boundary with Louisiana. The future of freshwater fishing in Texas is bright. Modern management techniques combined with a long growing season, productive watersheds, and the growth of conservation measures such as catch-and-release fishing bodes well for the continuation of great fishing in the Lone Star State for generations to come.

This book is designed to provide anglers a useful reference for the best places to fish in Texas. That is, of course, a subjective goal because each site has its own character and reputation. Many of them are very similar in nature based upon the dominant species and ecological zones where they are found. Every attempt has been made to provide accurate and relevant information on a site-by-site basis. I have fished many of them over the three decades I have lived in Texas. Information presented is from my own personal experiences, the knowledge of fishing friends, and the many guides I have known who fish their respective lakes nearly every day. Fishery biologists from the Texas Parks and Wildlife Department have also contributed greatly to this book. Their knowledge of the lakes and rivers in their areas of responsibility is based upon scientific research and living and working among the anglers who frequent the sites in their districts.

The key elements in selecting a site to fish that maximizes opportunity are based upon knowing where to go, the habitat requirements of individual species, understanding their biological processes, and being able to interpret how seasonal influences impact the chances to catch them. Knowing all that is still no guarantee of being in the right place at the right time, but it helps. As one of my fishing buddies used to say after catching a particularly nice fish, "I would rather be lucky than good."

History

Largemouth bass are the number-one gamefish in Texas according to surveys compiled by the Texas Parks and Wildlife Department. And much of the focus on fishing in Texas is devoted to pursuit of the largemouth bass. For all practical purposes the history of Texas fishing began in 1943 when H. R. Magee caught a largemouth bass in Lake Medina that weighed 13.5 pounds and was 28.75 inches long. Medina is a small water-supply reservoir located northwest of San Antonio in the Hill Country region of the state. That record lasted for thirty-seven years and would more than likely still be in force if not for new management strategies implemented by state fishery officials.

Bob Kemp was the hatchery manager of the Tyler State Fish Hatchery in the 1970s and was convinced that the Florida strain of largemouth bass would outgrow the native Texas largemouth. He wanted to import some of them from Florida and see if his hypothesis was correct. Upper management did not share his views, so Kemp spent his own money to import 2,000 Florida fingerlings and had them shipped to Tyler, Texas, in 1971. In 1972 he also obtained 411 Florida brood bass. Kemp spawned the bass and was able to place 10,000 Florida fingerlings in Lake Murval located in Panola County in East Texas that same year. That event was the beginning of modern bass fishing in Texas and it would eventually catapult the state to the top of the bass-fishing world.

The chance to catch a largemouth bass weighing 10 pounds or more is a realistic goal for anglers who come to Texas. Bass in the 7- to 9-pound range rarely even raise an eyebrow among native Texans these days. Largemouth bass fishing is big business and opportunities to catch trophy fish from public water bodies abound. Florida-strain bass have been stocked into just about every reservoir that has suitable habitat across the state.

But the excellent largemouth bass fishing is just part of the story. Three species of catfish, two of crappie, striped bass, white bass, and their hybrids are also abundant. Other species of black bass such as the smallmouth, the Kentucky bass, and the Guadalupe bass, a unique native species, are available to anglers. Red drum are a hard-fighting coastal species with a tolerance for freshwater much like the striped bass, and they have been stocked in certain freshwater lakes that provide suitable habitat. Trout are also stocked into small lakes scattered across the state during the winter. The Guadalupe River immediately below Canyon Lake Dam in central Texas supports a year-round trout fishery that is very popular with fly-fishing enthusiasts. Texas also has a small walleye fishery in Lake Meredith located in the Texas Panhandle north of Amarillo. Giant gamefish—Texas has them. The state record for largemouth bass is 18.18 pounds, for blue catfish 121.5 pounds, and striped bass is 53 pounds, just to name a few. If catching numbers of fish is the quest, Texas can provide that too with lakes and rivers that brim with crappie, catfish, white bass, and sunfish. The opportunities are nearly limitless.

Major Fishing Programs

One of the most recognized and successful fishery programs in Texas is the Toyota ShareLunker Program. It officially began in 1986 when a local East Texas guide by the name of Mark Stevenson caught a largemouth bass from Lake Fork that weighed 17.67 pounds and donated it—alive—to fishery officials from Texas Parks and Wildlife's Inland Fisheries Division. It was at that time the largest bass ever caught in Texas. State biologists had been toying with the idea of initiating a program that would increase public awareness of just how good bass fishing had become in Texas and that the opportunity to catch a giant bass was a reality, not just a concept. Officials were also seeking a means to improve the fishing public's awareness of how important it was to release bass, especially the large females, for the future health of the bass fishery in Texas. Stevenson's catch validated those concepts and began what would become a milestone in fishery management in Texas.

The original program as it was conceived was to encourage anglers who caught bass that weighed 13 pounds or more during the cool-water months to donate them alive to biologists who would then stabilize and study the fish and try to get them to spawn under controlled hatchery conditions. The idea was to use these "super bass" to improve the genetics of hatchery brood stock for largemouth bass stocking programs in Texas. After study and spawning, the bass and a significant portion of their fry would be released back into the water body from which they were caught. Another component of the program was to document and publicize the importance of releasing large bass because they are the most prolific egg layers. The larger the female bass, the more eggs she can lay.

Anglers who donate are rewarded with statewide media attention, a life-size replica of their bass, promotional clothing, and an invitation to attend an annual banquet where they are feted for their donation and accomplishment.

The program has been wildly successful. During the past twenty-six years, 525 largemouth bass weighing 13 pounds or more have been entered. They were caught from fifty-five public reservoirs representing all ecological regions of Texas. The size of the state record bass has increased from 13.5 pounds—a fish caught from previously mentioned Lake Medina in 1943—to the current record of 18.18 pounds caught in 1992 from Lake Fork in East Texas. Qualifying for the ShareLunker Program has become the Holy Grail for bass fishermen in Texas. The program's concept of publicizing the excellent opportunity to catch trophy-sized fish and how important catch-and-release is to the continuation of that abundance has been realized. Texas anglers can boast they have the best bass fishing in the nation and biologists have the scientific data to back it up.

On June 2, 1932, George Perry caught a largemouth bass from Montgomery Lake in Georgia that weighed 22.4 pounds. That bass has been the official world record for the species for the past seventy-nine years. Perry's catch is considered to be one of the most prestigious and sought-after of all freshwater fishing records.

Operation World Record is an offshoot of the ShareLunker Program, with the lofty goal of producing a bass in Texas that can eclipse Perry's long-standing record. Biologists are pairing pure Florida-strain ShareLunker bass in a selective breeding process. The goal is to produce bass that have the genetic capability to grow fast, get large, and survive long enough to reach the 22.4-pound mark and beyond. Offspring from the lunker bass spawned in a controlled environment are implanted with a tag that can be scanned electronically. They are then stocked into small impoundments scattered across the state. Biologists will periodically capture the young bass and monitor their growth and survival rates. This program is revolutionary in that the effectiveness of a selective breeding program for the sole purpose of developing a fish that can achieve record sizes has not been proven scientifically. According to biologists, it will take at least ten years of continued effort and monitoring to determine if the process will provide results that might achieve the program's goal. The current state-record bass of 18.18 pounds was determined to be 10 to 11 years old when caught in 1992. Based upon age data collected from the ShareLunker Program bass over the past twenty years, it takes at least eight to ten years of growth to achieve an average weight of 13 pounds. Biologists theorize that in order to reach world-record size, a selectively bred bass will require at least ten years of growth.

Catch-and-Release

The catch-and-release concept in Texas began with the realization that no resource has inexhaustible limits. The roots of that discovery came in the early 1970s when anglers began to notice that the quantity and quality of bass fishing in Texas was declining. Ask any bass angler in the 1960s if it was possible to overfish a huge reservoir like 114,000-acre Sam Rayburn, located in southeast Texas, and they would laugh and shake their heads. But by the next decade, heavy fishing pressure and liberal daily bag limits were taking a toll. Bass fishing in Texas was on a downward spiral.

Fishery biologists took notice and began to experiment with new management techniques on small lakes. From the data they collected during those initial experiments, they found it was possible to improve the quantity and quality of bass by implementing new restrictions. They were convinced the same strategy would work on large impoundments too. As a result of their efforts, management plans were developed that included limiting the number and size of fish that could be retained by anglers daily. This pioneering work led to new regulations promoting the modern concept of catch-and-release bass fishing.

The catch-and-release concept got a big boost in the 1980s with the development of the ShareLunker Program mentioned earlier. That program provided outdoor media with a platform to encourage anglers to release bass in order to give them a chance to grow to lunker size.

Angler Recognition

So you caught a fish. Ever wonder if it might qualify for a record? Mention record fish to most folks and images of a fuzzy photo in a local paper showing a tired but happy angler trying their best to hold up a huge fish comes to mind. That pretty much used to be the case, but Texas Parks and Wildlife's Angler Recognition Program has changed all that.

Lake records and state records have been kept for many years in an "unofficial status." But starting in the 1980s, Texas Parks and Wildlife began a program recognizing anglers who catch record fish.

Catching a water body or state record fish has never been an easy task to accomplish. Very few fish live long enough to achieve the necessary size. The odds of catching a state or water body record are long even for veteran anglers. How do you allow more anglers to have a shot at catching record fish? The solution was to create more categories.

The Angler Recognition Program now consists of several categories that allow beginning-to-seasoned anglers to be "in the book." Following are the categories and the requirements necessary for submitting an application.

Is there a record fish out there with your name on it? Creating all of these categories for angler recognition has greatly increased the odds in favor of fishermen to "put one in the book."

Application forms, rules, and qualifying species are available from the Program Coordinator for Inland Fisheries at (512) 389-8031 or by e-mail at anglers@tpwd .state.tx.us. Many marinas and bait stores also have copies of Angler Recognition applications and rules of entry. Complete rules and award categories are also available from the Texas Parks and Wildlife Department headquarters at 4200 Smith School Rd., Austin, TX 78744. Call (800) 792-1112 or visit www.tpwd.state.tx.us, click on Fishing, and follow the links.

State Records

Two categories exist for this most prestigious record, one for public waters and one for private. Allowable means of capture on public waters are rod and reel, fly fishing, unrestricted (this includes trotlines and jug lines), and bow fishing. For private waters the unrestricted means is eliminated.

Water Body Records

Three categories exist for this award: all tackle (the largest fish caught by any legal method), fly fishing (the largest fish caught using artificial flies), and bow fishing.

Big Fish Award

Realizing that a trophy fish does not have to be a state or water body record fish, a new award category called simply Big Fish Award was created. This category acknowledges anglers who catch trophy fish and want to be recognized for it. Minimum length requirements were created by field biologists and weighing is required for selected freshwater species. Fish must be weighed, on certified scales, within three days of being caught. This award is also given to anglers who catch selected saltwater species. The weighing requirement is optional for this category. Complete lists of fresh- and saltwater species that qualify for this award and the minimum lengths for each are available from the program coordinator or by calling Texas Parks and Wildlife Department headquarters in Austin.

Catch-and-Release Award

In a tribute to anglers who have voluntarily adopted a catch-and-release ethic for trophy fish, TPWD has introduced an award that recognizes them. Fish entered in this category must meet or exceed a certain length. Anglers are required to measure and photograph the fish and must have a witness present. Qualifying species are the same as for the Big Fish Award. Two categories are available: rod and reel and fly fishing.

Elite Angler Award

This one recognizes anglers who catch five trophy-sized fish in a lifetime. To receive this recognition, an angler must possess five Big Fish Awards.

First Fish Award

This category recognizes catching that first fish as a very important milestone in the development of young or adult anglers.

Outstanding Angler Award

The next step up from a First Fish Award, this category recognizes anglers who catch fish that do not meet the requirements for other awards.

State Catch-and-Release Record

This award is for the catch and live release of the longest fish of a qualifying species from Texas public waters.

Catch-and-Release Water Body Record

To qualify for this category, an angler must catch and live release the longest fish of a qualifying species from a public water body.

Major Species

Largemouth Bass

Description: Largemouth bass are predominately green on the back and sides, overlaid with dark, irregular spots that tend to form a dark stripe down each side of the body. The belly is white or cream colored. One identifying characteristic to distinguish them from other of the so-called black basses is the upper jaw, which extends well beyond the large eyes. They are also known as black bass, bigmouth bass, and in some parts of the state, green trout. Their dorsal fin is nearly divided into two sections. The front portion contains nine sharp spines and the rear, twelve or thirteen soft rays. They can live as long as twelve to fifteen years, though six years is average.

   Habitat: Largemouth bass prefer quiet, slightly stained water with a large amount of vegetation. In lakes without adequate aquatic plants, they will live near rocks, logs, standing flooded timber, or man-made structure including boat docks, bridges, and marinas. They are an adaptable species and can maintain adequate populations in just about any habitat that provides the minimum amount of forage and cover. But the best lakes to fish for them are those with a substantial variety of vegetative cover.

Distribution: Fair to excellent populations are present in all geographical regions of Texas with adequate habitat.

Special notes: The northern strain of largemouth bass is native to Texas and has been widely stocked into ponds and reservoirs for many decades. In the 1970s fishery biologists imported the Florida-strain largemouth bass from the southeastern United States and stocked them into select reservoirs in East Texas. The species prospered and revolutionized Texas bass fishing. Previous to stocking Florida bass, the largest bass ever officially recorded weighed 13.5 pounds, a record that lasted for thirty-seven years. In 1980 the record was broken by a Florida-strain bass that topped 14 pounds. In the ensuing eleven years, that record was broken repeatedly, until 1992 when Barry St.Clair caught a largemouth bass from Lake Fork that weighed 18.18 pounds. It still stands as the largest bass ever caught in Texas and was ranked by the International Game Fish Association as the second-largest bass caught in the United States that year. Biologists have found that the Florida strain is better suited to the giant impoundments in Texas and quickly grows to large sizes. Florida bass have since been stocked into many impoundments in all geographical regions of the state that have adequate habitat.

Smallmouth Bass

Description: As its name suggests, the smallmouth bass is more refined and streamlined than its cousin the largemouth. The upper jaw does not extend past the eye. Coloration varies with age, but the body is primarily a brown, gold, and green combination with vertical dark bands that can be prominent or light along the length of the fish's body. The dorsal fin consists of thirteen to fifteen soft rays. One of their colloquial names is red-eye in reference to the large amount of red coloring in the iris. The underside is yellowish to creamy white.

Habitat: Smallmouth bass thrive best in large clear-water lakes at least 30 feet deep with rock or gravel bottoms. They are ideally suited to river habitats with spring-fed water sources and rocky streambeds.

Distribution: Smallmouth bass are not native to Texas but have been stocked into various reservoirs and rivers across the state. The bass are not widespread but through periodic stockings by the Texas Parks and Wildlife Department, fishable populations are maintained in reservoirs and streams in the Hill Country, Panhandle Plains, and Big Bend regions of Texas.

Special notes: Smallmouth bass are strong, acrobatic fighters, and they have a small but enthusiastic following among Texas anglers. The state record is held by a fish caught from Lake Meredith in the Panhandle Plains region in 1998 that weighed 7.93 pounds. The previous record came from Lake Whitney in the Hill Country region. Crayfish, small minnows, and aquatic insect larvae are their preferred food sources. Small crankbaits, jigs, and plastic creature baits are the most popular lures used to catch them.

Spotted Bass

Description: Spotted bass are also known as Kentucky bass and spotted black bass. They have similar coloration to the largemouth bass except for the pattern of dark markings along their sides below the lateral line, which are arranged in rows of black dots. Other distinguishing marks include a red-orange iris, chalky- or cream-colored belly, and a small mouth, the lower jaw of which does not extend past the eye. Dorsal fin separations are less clearly defined than the largemouth. They are similar in habits to the smallmouth, and hybrids between the species are not unusual where their ranges overlap.

Habitat: Spotted bass fill habitat niches between the largemouth and small-mouth basses. They prefer more current than does the largemouth and are quite at home in rivers and streams too warm for smallmouth bass. They do well in deep-water reservoirs of the South that contain gravel and rock bottoms.

Distribution: Spotted bass are a native species in Texas and are found primarily in reservoirs and streams in the eastern third of the state from the Guadalupe River to the Red River.

Special notes: Even though spotted bass do not achieve the size of the large-mouth, they are known as a hard-fighting species and much prized by anglers in East Texas. Excellent populations are present in the Neches, Sabine, and Cypress Rivers as well as most of the large reservoirs in the eastern Piney Woods region. The state record fish weighed 5.56 pounds and was caught from Lake o' the Pines. Spotted bass have a diet similar to the smallmouth, and they readily strike lures that resemble crayfish and small minnows.

Guadalupe Bass

Description: To the untrained eye the Guadalupe bass looks much like a smallmouth or spotted bass, but there are some key indications that separate their distinguish-ing characteristics. The body is green-gold with irregular black splotches scattered along the sides and back without any vertical orientation like the smallmouth. The dark spots extend much further down the sides of the fish's body than the spotted bass. These are small river-oriented fish that rarely exceed 1 to 2 pounds in weight.

Habitat: Guadalupe bass are a river species and prefer small streams with fast currents and rocky substrate bottoms.

Distribution: The Guadalupe bass is a true Texas native and it is found in the clear-water streams of the Hill Country region in central Texas. This region includes the Colorado, Guadalupe, and San Antonio River drainages of the Edwards Plateau. They do best in rivers with fast currents and clean water, feeding primarily on crus-taceans, minnows, and insect larvae. They are present in the impounded reservoirs of the region but generally in small numbers.

Special notes: The range of the Guadalupe bass lies entirely in Texas, and as a result they have been proclaimed the official state fish. Smallmouth bass were stocked into much of the Guadalupe's habitat and it was later found they would readily interbreed with the Guadalupe. This threatened the pure strain of the native fish, and once this was determined to be the case, stocking of the smallmouth in historical Guadalupe habitat was discontinued. The Guadalupe bass is a favorite target of fly fishermen because of the small, scenic streams they inhabit and their willingness to take flies that resemble aquatic insects and small minnows. The state record for this small but scrappy member of the black basses is 3.69 pounds and was caught from Lake Travis in the Hill Country region.

White Bass

Description: White bass are members of the temperate, or true, bass family. Their dorsal fins are separated into a spiny front lobe and soft-rayed rear appendage. Coloration is silvery gray on the back and silver-white on the sides, with faint to fairly prominent dark lines along the sides that rarely run uninterrupted the entire length of the body. Bellies are white. Often confused with juvenile striped bass when they inhabit the same water body, white bass have one distinct tooth patch on the back of their tongues, while striped bass have two. The back edges of white bass gill plates are very sharp and sport one distinctive point; striped bass have two. Their species name, *chrysops,* is a Greek word meaning golden eye, referring to the light to medium yellow color of the iris. White bass grow rapidly and can achieve a mature weight of 1 to 2 pounds in two years. Any white bass over 3 pounds is considered a trophy.

  Habitat: White bass are home in rivers and reservoirs with hard bottoms of sand, gravel, or rock. They are a schooling fish and spend most of their lives in open water areas of large reservoirs chasing their favorite forage species, threadfin and gizzard shad. During late winter and early spring, they migrate up tributaries to spawn. In rivers they will be found in the deeper pools.

  Distribution: White bass are native in Texas to the Red River and its tributaries along the northern and eastern boundaries of the state. They have been widely stocked into most rivers and reservoirs across the state that have adequate habitat.

  Special notes: White bass provide one of the most popular and dependable fisheries in Texas. Their genetically programmed trait of running up rivers and streams to spawn has earned them the nickname Texas salmon. Thousands of fish move out of reservoirs into tributaries to complete their reproductive rites starting as early as December in South Texas and continuing until mid-April in the northern regions of the state. This event is eagerly anticipated by winter-weary anglers. White bass will voraciously attack small spoons, jigs, and spinners, and liberal daily limits and their willingness to bite make them an ideal sport fish for anglers of all abilities. The state record white bass was caught from the Colorado River in central Texas and weighed 5.56 pounds. Most Texans refer to white bass as sand bass, a colloquialism that refers to the white bass's penchant for spawning on sandy points of land.

Striped Bass

Description: Striped bass are the largest member of the true, or temperate, bass family. They are silvery gray on the sides, fading to a light, translucent green on the back, with a white underbelly. Seven to eight continuous black lines run the length of their sides. Gill flaps have two sharp points, and there are two distinctive tooth patches on their tongues. Dorsal fins are separate and arrayed into a spiny-rayed front and soft-rayed rear. Striped bass grow rapidly and can achieve 12-inch lengths in one year. They are aggressive open water predators that tend to stay together in schools of the same year class. Their Latin-derived species name, *saxatilis,* means rock dweller, which refers to their penchant for living near rocky structure.

Habitat: Striped bass are an introduced species in Texas. They were first stocked into selected reservoirs in the 1960s. They do best in river-fed reservoirs with cool, clear water and rocky-substrate bottoms with depths to 100 feet.

Distribution: Striped bass populations are currently being maintained in sixteen reservoirs scattered across the state. These fisheries are periodically restocked because reservoir systems in Texas do not meet their reproductive needs. Stripers need large rivers with adequate flow, salinity levels, and length to keep their eggs in suspension for thirty-six to seventy-two hours in order for them to hatch into fry. Only Lake Texoma, on the northern border with Oklahoma in the Prairies and Lakes region, supports a naturally reproducing fishery for striped bass in Texas.

Special notes: Striped bass are anadromous. Adults live in salt water and migrate up freshwater rivers that flow into the Atlantic Ocean and the Gulf of Mexico to spawn. It was not until the 1940s that biologists discovered that striped bass could successfully live in a freshwater environment year-round. This adaptive quality allowed them to be stocked in many lakes and establish an outstanding new species for inland fishermen to enjoy. They are one of the most popular gamefish in Texas, and many local economies depend on the anglers that fish exclusively for them. Their primary food sources are threadfin and gizzard shad. These species are abundant in the large open water reservoirs where stripers are stocked in Texas. Favorite tactics to catch them include using live bait, trolling, jigging, and when they are feeding on shad on the surface, large top-water lures. Stripers can achieve great sizes. The Texas record is 53 pounds—the fish was caught in the Brazos River below the dam on Possum Kingdom Reservoir in the Panhandle Plains region.

Hybrid Striped Bass

Description: The hybrid striped bass is a cross between the striped bass and the white bass. Hybrids have the body shape of a white bass but grow much larger. They sport silvery gray sides shading to pearlescent green on the back. Bellies are white and dorsal fins are separate. The familiar dark lines on the sides found on both parent species are typically broken and irregular on the rear third of the flank of the hybrid. But not all hybrids are so marked. Most hybrids have two tooth patches on the tongue, but not always. These inconsistencies make them easily confused with white bass. Hybrids grow rapidly and can reach 18 inches in length in three seasons. Typical life expectancy is five or six years and they can easily reach 8 to 10 pounds. They are incapable of reproducing, so populations must be maintained through regular stocking programs by the state.

Habitat: Hybrids are more heat tolerant than striped bass and can be stocked in shallower, more turbid reservoirs than the striper. They also do well in the cool, clear water stripers prefer.

Distribution: 8.7 million hybrid stripers have been stocked into an average of thirteen Texas reservoirs by state fishery crews in 2010. These lakes are primarily located in the Hill Country and Prairies and Lakes regions.

Special notes: Hybrid striped bass are an aggressive gamefish that incorporate the best features of their parent species. They are primarily an open water schooling fish that roams reservoirs pursuing threadfin shad. They thrive in semi-turbid water and have a tendency to feed on or near the surface as white bass do. They grow to large sizes like striped bass and put up a remarkable battle when hooked. Anglers who pursue them claim they fight harder than any other freshwater gamefish. When surface feeding they greedily strike shad-imitating top-water lures. Hybrids gang up into large schools and suspend on creek channels and underwater humps when they are not active on the surface. Anglers have good success in fishing for them with slabs bounced off the bottom or dropping live bait down to just above their position in the water column. Trolling silver spoons and white-hair jigs are also productive techniques. The Texas record is 19.66 pounds and was caught from Lake Ray Hubbard, which is located in the Prairies and Lakes region of Texas.

Channel Catfish

Description: Channel catfish are perhaps the most identifiable of the catfish family. Their coloration is variable, ranging from dark to light gray on the back with a hint of blue. Bellies are silvery-white. Juveniles typically have a sprinkling of random black spots along the sides. The tail fin is deeply forked. Pectoral fins and the dorsal each have one long sharp spine. The most identifiable characteristics that separate them from the similar blue catfish are the number of soft rays in the anal fin and its shape. Channel catfish have twenty-four to twenty-nine rays, and the fin is rounded on the bottom edge. Blues have thirty to thirty-five rays in their anal fins, and the bottom edge is angular.

Habitat: Channel catfish are historically a river fish. They do well in bodies of water with current and prefer streams and reservoirs with clear water and rocky bottoms. But they are an adaptable species and will prosper in water that exhibits some seasonal turbidity.

Distribution: The channel catfish is native to Texas rivers and has been stocked into most public water bodies. They are present in all regions of the state that have adequate habitat to support them.

Special notes: Channel catfish have a wide following among Texas anglers and are the second-most sought-after gamefish in the state according to surveys conducted by state fishery crews. They grow rapidly and feed all year long in the southern portions of the state. Angling for them is easy as they will readily bite just about any type of bait. They are primarily a scavenger but will readily take small lures and flies too. Their reproductive capabilities keep their natural populations high, which leads to high catch rates for anglers. They are a preferred food fish by the anglers who pursue them. Catfish are scrappy fighters when hooked, adding to their appeal. Channel catfish exceeding 10 pounds are common and they can grow to large sizes. The state record weighed 36.5 pounds and was caught from the Perdernales River in the Hill Country region.

Blue Catfish

Description: Blue catfish are similar in appearance to channel catfish, with slate-gray backs shading to a white belly. Anal fins contain thirty to thirty-five soft rays, and the bottom edge of the fin is angular, not rounded. The tail fin is also deeply forked. Their species name, *furcatus,* is Latin meaning "forked." They are the largest of the catfish species and grow to more than 100 pounds. Typically, trophy fish are considered anything above 30 pounds.

Habitat: Blues are historically river fish, preferring deep holes with current, but also do well in large reservoirs on major river systems with fairly clear water. They are native to Texas rivers in the eastern half of the state.

Distribution: Blue catfish have been widely stocked into many city and urban lakes as well as large rural water bodies across the state.

Special notes: Catch-and-release fishing for trophy-sized blue catfish has become popular in Texas. Guides have learned how to catch these largest of the catfishes and encourage anglers who do so to release them. Trophy-sized blues of 40 to 60 pounds are not uncommon in many Texas reservoirs. The state record blue catfish in Texas was caught from Lake Texoma in the Prairies and Lakes region by an angler in 2004. That fish weighed 121.5 pounds and was the world record for the species on rod and reel until a 124-pound fish was caught from the Mississippi River a year later. Most large blues are caught in the winter, when they have a tendency to feed during the day and gang up under schools of baitfish that have moved to deep-water structure to survive the cold water temperatures.

Flathead Catfish

Description: Flatheads are the pit bulls of the catfish world. They even resemble them, with an undershot jaw, mottled brown and yellow body coloration, and a junkyard-dog attitude if you cross them. Their bellies are usually pale yellow with traces of gray. The tail fin is slightly lobed and their flattened heads give them their name. Their scientific name, *Pylodictis olivaris,* means olive-colored mudfish in Latin. Common names for them include yellow cat, shovelhead, and Opelousa. They are the second-largest catfish species and can attain weights of over 100 pounds. Flatheads are solitary as adults and, unlike other catfish species, almost exclusively prefer live prey. They are primarily nocturnal and feed on other fish including carp, drum, shad, and sunfish.

Habitat: Flatheads are native to Texas rivers. They prefer deep pools or channels with turbid water and slow currents. Tailrace areas below dams are prime locations to find them.

Distribution: Flatheads are widely distributed in Texas and can be found in most water bodies capable of supporting their live prey preferences. They do especially well in the larger rivers and reservoirs located in the eastern half of Texas.

Special notes: It takes three to six years for flatheads to reach sexual maturity. To compensate for their slow growth, restrictive size limits have been introduced to protect them from being overharvested. A flathead must be at least 18 inches in length to retain, and the bag limit is five per day per angler. There is no maximum size restriction. Their nocturnal nature makes them a challenge for rod-and-reel anglers and so most large flatheads are caught on jug or trot lines left baited over-night. But there is a dedicated core of anglers that fish for them with rod and reel as they put up a great battle when hooked. Fishing river or lake flats in the evening with a live 5- to 6-inch shad, carp, or sunfish as bait suspended under a float is one preferred method. Fresh cut bait fished on the bottom in tailrace areas or deep holes in rivers is another means of catching them. The state rod-and-reel record weighed 98.5 pounds and was caught by an angler fishing for crappie under a bridge on Lake Palestine in the Piney Woods region of East Texas.

Black Crappie

Description: Black crappies get their name from the prolific number of random black spots sprinkled liberally over their robust bodies. Coloration is a combination of silvery black and green. Their fins are large and also exhibit a large amount of black spotting. Dorsal fins have seven or eight sharp spines and the opercle flap located at the rear of the gill plate has two sharp points. They commonly reach 12 inches in length and 1 to 1.25 pounds in weight. Larger fish are not common but they can grow to 6 pounds.

 Habitat: Black crappies prefer clear, tannin-colored acidic water with firm bottoms that predominates eastern Texas rivers and reservoirs.

 Distribution: This popular species is native to central and eastern Texas rivers. They have been widely stocked in most man-made reservoirs in those regions.

 Special notes: Black crappies are prized as a food fish by anglers, who pursue them with a passion for their delicate flavor. They are nest builders and move to very shallow water in the spring to spawn. This characteristic makes them available in large numbers to anglers along the banks of rivers and reservoirs. They will readily strike small jigs and minnows. Because of their strong reproductive ability and widespread distribution, limits are liberal. The daily bag limit is twenty-five fish per person and they must be 10 inches in length to keep. After the spawning season they retreat to deeper water and form large schools. They have an affinity for woody structure and commonly congregate in areas of flooded timber along creek channels in 12 to 20 feet of water. The state record weighed 3.92 pounds and was caught from Lake Fork in 2003 in the Piney Woods region of East Texas.

White Crappie

Description: White crappies are easily distinguished from black crappies by their lighter body colors and a series of dark vertical bands on their sides extending to the tail. The Latin species name of *annularis* is a direct reference to this coloration. Sides are silvery white, shading to an iridescent purple-green on the back. They are deep-bodied and the dorsal fin contains no more than six sharp spines. The name "crappie" is thought to be derived from the French Canadian word for pancake, *crapet,* a reference to the outline of a crappie fillet, which roughly resembles a pancake. Body shape is more elongated than that of the black crappie. They become mature in two to three years and commonly reach sizes of 12 to 13 inches and weights of 1 to 1.5 pounds.

 Habitat: A common name for this species in many parts of its range is timber crappie. This is because of the white crappie's affinity for living in and near flooded trees and submerged brush. They are more tolerant of turbid water than black crappie. In early spring they move into flooded woodlands in very shallow water to spawn. After their reproductive rites are complete, they relocate to deeper water and can be found in large groups around boat docks, along flooded creek channels with timber, and man-made brush piles.

Distribution: White crappies are native to river systems in the eastern two-thirds of Texas and have been widely stocked into most man-made reservoirs across the state.

Special notes: Crappies are ranked in the top three of most desirable species sought by anglers in Texas. Only the largemouth bass and catfish outrank them. One reason for this is that during their spring spawning season, they become easily accessible to both bank and boat anglers when they move to shallow areas to build nests and lay eggs. Dabbling a small minnow or jig in front of nesting fish will quickly generate a strike. Limits are liberal with a size restriction of 10 inches minimum length and a maximum of twenty-five fish per angler per day. White crappies are considered to be a delicacy for their firm, sweet flesh. Crappies are easily attracted to woody structure and many enthusiasts build their own crappie condominiums by sinking brush and small trees into desirable areas around boat docks and along creek channels. The state rod-and-reel record is 4.56 pounds. The fish was caught from Navarro Lake in the Prairies and Lakes region.

Red Drum (Redfish)

Description: Red drum are known as redfish in Texas and are a saltwater species that, like the striped bass, can adapt to certain freshwater environments that meet their needs. They are in the same family as the common freshwater drum. The name reflects their color, which can range from a silvery copper to a reddish bronze. The mouth is pointed downward like other drums due to their bottom-feeding nature. One of their distinguishing characteristics is one or several black spots about the size of a dime on the upper region of their tail base. Scales are large and they have no barbells on the lower mouth. They grow rapidly and can achieve sizes of 6 to 8 pounds in three years. Like other members of the drum family, redfish can generate a booming sound by manipulating their swim bladder. The reason for this behavior is unknown. They are an aggressive predator and will strike artificial lures and flies, but most are caught using fresh or cut bait fished on the bottom.

Habitat: Redfish are primarily associated with coastal bays in Texas. They can survive and grow to large sizes in freshwater lakes with high concentrations of dissolved minerals that are artificially heated by electric power generation.

Distribution: Four lakes in Texas make up the majority of inland redfish habitat. They are Lakes Calaveras and Braunig in the South Texas Plains region and Lake Fairfield and Tradinghouse Creek Reservoir in the Prairies and Lakes region. One and a half million redfish were stocked in 2010 and 1.3 million in 2011 by state fishery crews. Other lakes in the state have been stocked, but populations are not viable due to ongoing environmental conditions such as drought and golden algae outbreaks. These limiting factors are detailed in later sections of this book.

Special notes: Fishing for redfish in freshwater lakes comprises a small percentage of angling opportunities in Texas, but it has an enthusiastic following. Redfish are known for their scrappy hard fight when hooked and can achieve large sizes. They are primarily bottom feeders but readily attack minnow-imitating lures and shiny spoons. Since they cannot reproduce in freshwater environments, regular stocking is required to maintain adequate populations. The state record for redfish is 36.83 pounds and it was caught from Lake Fairfield in the Prairies and Lakes region in 2001.

Rainbow Trout

Description: Rainbow trout are easily recognized by their olive-colored backs, heavily speckled bodies, and broad pink stripe running the length of each side. Their body shape is streamlined. Scales are small and the anal fin has ten to twelve soft rays.

Habitat: These members of the salmon family are most comfortable in clear, rocky-bottomed streams and reservoirs where water temperatures remain below 70 degrees F. They exist in Texas seasonally due to the high summer water temperatures common to the state, with one major exception noted below. The only self-propagating population of rainbow trout in Texas is located in McKittrick Canyon, in the Guadalupe Mountains in the southwest corner of the Panhandle Plains region.

Distribution: Rainbow trout are primarily a winter put-and-take fishery in Texas. The major exception is the Guadalupe River tailrace below Canyon Reservoir in the Hill Country region of central Texas. Several miles of river habitat supports a year-round fishery below the dam because the discharge from this reservoir releases cold water from the bottom of the impoundment. The state, along with the Guadalupe River Trout Unlimited Chapter, heavily stocks this section of the river on an annual basis. Otherwise, the Texas Parks and Wildlife Department stocks approximately one hundred sites in Texas from December through March to increase angling opportunities for catching these popular fish. Most of these locations are small city, municipal, and state park lakes within or close to major urban areas. Sites and dates stocked for the latest season are available online at www.tpwd.state.tx.us.

Special notes: Rainbow trout in Texas offer winter angling opportunities for a species that is easy to catch and thrives in cold water. Unlike native warmwater species such as largemouth bass and catfish, trout continue to feed regularly when water temperatures plummet in the winter. They readily bite small baits including whole kernel corn, prepared dough baits, and small worms. This makes them ideal candidates for young anglers and novice adults. They do retain some of the characteristics of their wild brethren and will strike small spinners and flies. Adding to their popularity is the bag limit of five per person per day and no size restrictions. The state record was caught on a red wiggler worm from the Guadalupe River below Canyon Reservoir in 2001 and weighed 8.24 pounds.

Walleye

Description: Walleye are a member of the perch family with distinctive large eyes with hazy or glassy pupils that give them their common name of walleyed perch. The retinas contain a special crystal-like material that reflects light in order for them to be a sight predator in the low-light environments they prefer. Dorsal fins are completely separated, with the front fin bearing sharp spines while the rear fin is soft with twelve to fourteen rays. The anal fin is also barbed. Coloration is green-yellow-brown with irregular black splotches on the sides. Their body shape is elongated. The lower jaw and roof of their mouths are studded with sharp teeth. Adults prey primarily on other fish.

Habitat: Walleye do best in deep coldwater environments with rocky substrate bottoms. They are not native to Texas but have been introduced into a few reservoirs in the northwest part of the state that provides those conditions. Typically walleye achieve weights of 5 to 8 pounds in Texas. Warm water temperatures present during the summer season limits their ability to grow much larger.

Distribution: Since 2000 approximately 8.4 million walleye fingerlings have been stocked into four Texas lakes in the Panhandle Plains region by Texas Parks and Wildlife Department fishery crews. Those lakes are Meredith, Palo Duro, White River, and Greenbelt.

Special notes: Lake Meredith, 45 miles north of Amarillo, provides the best walleye fishing in Texas. The lake has documented natural reproduction and enough area and depth to provide an ongoing quality fishery. Walleye are spring spawners and move up tributaries and onto rocky, shallow flats to reproduce. April to June is the best time of the year to catch them out of their deep-water haunts. Small crankbaits, jigs, spoons, and plastic creature baits are good lure choices. Fish lures slowly for best results. Minnows and crawfish are the best live baits. Walleye are most active in low-light situations so early and late is the favored time to fish for them. During the day they retreat to deep-water ledges and humps. The state record walleye weighed 11.8 pounds and was caught from Lake Meredith.

Stocking

Texas Parks and Wildlife fishery crews stock millions of fish in public freshwater lakes, ponds, and rivers every year. The greatest majority are largemouth bass and catfish, the two most popular species among anglers in the state. They are produced in hatcheries scattered across the state and then stocked primarily as fingerlings, sometimes as fry as time and space dictate. Some select fishery programs require adult fish to be stocked. These include the winter rainbow trout program and the Neighborhood Fishing Program, which stocks catchable-size fish into city and urban lakes for immediate harvest. Fish stocking programs are not designed to replace natural reproduction but rather supplement it when certain conditions exist. Fish are stocked to initiate populations in recently constructed water bodies, increase populations of select species that have inadequate reproduction due to natural or man-made conditions, introduce new species to appropriate habitat, provide harvest-size fish for special programs, or to more quickly take advantage of improved habitat conditions. For detailed contact information on water bodies and species stocked in Texas, see the appendix.

Limiting Factors

Drought

Devastating drought conditions throughout the state have resulted in the closure of many public boat ramps until further notice. While in many cases motorized vehicles are prohibited, small boats, canoes, and kayaks can still be launched from the shoreline at most locations. Lakes with limited access or consumption advisories as of press time are noted, but be sure to check with local lake authorities to get the latest update on conditions before you travel.

So many different climatic zones exist that it is difficult to find some area of the state not impacted in any given year by drought. In 2005 and 2006 most of the state was wrapped in a lingering dry period and many lakes experienced severe drawdowns. This had more of an impact on fishermen than fish as boating access became restricted and fishing pressure declined dramatically. The year 2007 saw a complete reverse of this trend in the eastern half of Texas as a normal year's worth of rainfall was recorded in the first six months. This caused torrential flooding of all major river basins in the affected areas. The good news is the downpours filled all reservoirs to the brim and beyond. That rainfall largess resulted in reestablishing the quality of fishing Texas is known to possess.

Golden alga is a microorganism present in Texas and is usually found in stagnant-to-brackish water. For reasons not clear to scientists, the normally harmless alga can at certain times grow very rapidly and become toxic to fish and other gill-breathing animals. This is known as a toxic alga bloom. Massive fish kills can be the result. The first documented case of a fish kill caused by a golden alga occurred on the Pecos River in the mid-1980s. Since then, other kills attributed to golden alga outbreaks have occurred in the Brazos, Canadian, Red River, and Colorado River watersheds. These occur primarily in the winter months and have affected several reservoir systems severely. Scientists are conducting ongoing research projects to try to understand the phenomenon and find mitigating measures to contain or control it. Currently, the only remedy for restoring an impacted fishery is restocking it. Contact information for the golden alga situation in Texas is available in the appendix.

Weather

Texas has its share of inclement weather: thunderstorms, hurricanes, and tornadoes are an ever-present possibility. The best advice toward avoiding serious weather-related consequences is to check forecasts and be prepared for sudden changes. The old adage "If you don't like the weather, just wait five minutes" is very accurate when discussing Texas weather. Every year anglers and boaters are caught unaware and unprepared for the rapid changes that can occur, and lives are needlessly lost. Lightning and strong winds are the usual culprits when it comes to impacting a day on the lake or river. Strong thunderstorms can erupt out of a seemingly endless blue sky without much notice.

One day in late spring, a friend and I were fishing for striped bass on Lake Tawakoni in the Prairies and Lakes region when a strong line of thunderstorms developed to the north. The sky quickly turned the color of ink. We were 2 miles from the nearest shelter and made a quick dash for the marina. Just as we tied up safely, the storm struck. The placid lake quickly turned into a maelstrom and bolts of lightning were striking everywhere. We took shelter under a storage shed as the rain pounded and wind blew in gusts up to 50 miles per hour. Other anglers were not so lucky. We watched helplessly as boats tried to reach the cove and safe harbor but were tossed up on the jetty rocks and sank. Luckily, the anglers got out of the water safely, but many had their boats damaged severely on the rocks or were sunk at the launch ramp. *Get off the water when thunderstorms are approaching.* Lightning can strike miles ahead of a storm and boats on open water are likely targets: The consequences can be fatal. Spring and summer are prime fishing times in Texas and those seasons are also when the greatest likelihood of strong storms is possible. Always carry emergency supplies including a weather radio to keep updated on local conditions.

Regulations

The Texas Parks and Wildlife Department publishes the *Outdoor Annual,* which contains complete fishing regulations. This publication is updated every year. Legal means, methods, and restrictions are listed for all public freshwater locations including exceptions to statewide regulations. Many bodies of water have specific rules and those are noted in an easy-to-understand table format. This publication is the legal reference for all anglers who fish in public waters. Copies are available where licenses are sold. There are approximately 2,000 locations statewide where licenses may be purchased. They are also available on the Internet. The web address is listed in the appendix. When fishing in Texas, an angler 17 years or older must carry, in addition to a fishing license, a driver's license or personal identification certificate issued by the state. Anglers 16 years old and younger are exempt from licensing requirements.

Access

Fishing access to public reservoirs is generally excellent for boaters in Texas. About 97 percent of Texas is private property and the shorelines of many reservoirs in the state fall into this category. Most reservoirs have multiple public and private boat ramps. Some are free, but many require a launch fee. Bank-fishing access is limited on most public reservoirs to areas within state, county, or city parks located on the lakes. Some private concessionaires offer pier, dock, or bank fishing for a fee. River access is more restrictive. Public fishing areas include the aforementioned parks and access sites along public roadways and bridges. Never assume a riverbank or lake shoreline is public property.

Fishery Management

For management purposes, Texas's freshwater fisheries are divided into three regions. These regions contain the seven zones outlined in this book. Management Region 1 contains the western half of the state including the Big Bend, Panhandle Plains, and South Texas Plains regions and approximately half of the Gulf Coast region. Management Region 2 includes the Hill Country region and part of the Prairies and Lakes region. Management Region 3 encompasses Piney Woods, Prairies and Lakes, and the upper half of the Gulf Coast region. Contact information for the regional and district biologists who oversee these management units are listed in the appendix. Part of their job is public information and they are the best source for details on the water bodies under their jurisdiction. Give them a call and they will be happy to help.

Locating Hot Spots

They exist on every water body: places where fish are found consistently and are almost always hungry and of sufficient size or numbers to make a grown angler nearly weep with joy when found. Secret spots that to the casual fisherman seem unremarkable, yet to those with a keen eye, they stand out as having characteristics that make them qualify as a hot spot.

But what do they look like? What characteristics do they share and how does one identify them? Those are the $64,000 questions, and finding the answers is what determines if a certain location has what it takes to reach the realm of consistent fish catching known as a hot spot.

Even the best hot spots are ephemeral—they change with astonishing regularity. Fish react quickly to changing weather systems and seasonal patterns. Places that are hot in the summer more than likely will be as lifeless as the moon in winter. So, rarely is there a spot on any water body that can produce great fishing all year round. With that bit of trivia held firmly in cheek, let's look at what constitutes a lake hot spot.

Fish have three basic requirements: food, shelter, and an escape route. Different species of fish have behavioral characteristics that determine where they are most likely to find their individual or group needs. Largemouth bass are primarily solitary ambush predators. They prefer to hide in locations that offer them easy access to their prey. Shorelines provide food, shelter, and escape cover for small forage species such as bluegill and threadfin shad, and that is why bass favor those areas too.

The rule of fishing for predatory species like largemouth bass is: Find the food and find the fish. But not just any shoreline area will do. Genuine largemouth bass hot spots offer just the right mix of feeding opportunities, shelter from other predators including man, and—of very high importance—a quick escape route to deep water and safety.

Points of land jutting into a main lake are likely hot spots for fish. Those with a creek channel that passes close to the shoreline and contains water at least 12 to 15 feet deep will have a resident bass population. Add in some vegetation and woody cover and that mix will produce ideal conditions for a hot spot. The plants will attract baitfish, the wood will offer protection, and the creek channel provides a handy escape route. Find a place that boasts those characteristics and fish it thoroughly. There will be bass somewhere in that location.

Coves off the main lake that have a tributary flowing into them are potential hot spots. If the creek maintains adequate depth of 8 to 12 feet for a few hundred yards or more, there will be bass in residence. They will be located in channel bends, especially those that contain either plants or woody cover, and along any weed beds on the edges of the creek channel. From those areas they will move up into the shallows toward the shoreline early and late in the day to forage. As the sun climbs into the sky, they will move back to the deeper water of the creek channel and safety.

Underwater islands, or humps as they are commonly referred to, are another place to locate large numbers of fish on a regular basis. Some forage species such as threadfin shad tend to spend much of their lives in more open water areas away from shorelines and the predators they contain. Shad will gather in large schools and seek safety in deeper water that also offers some form of structure. Underwater humps are shad magnets. Largemouth bass, catfish, and the temperate bass species, including white bass, striped bass, and hybrid striped bass, feed on shad. Finding an underwater hump with schools of shad hanging nearby is about as close to fishing nirvana as an angler can get. These areas typically harbor larger fish because of the abundant food available and the close proximity of deep-water escape routes.

Finding lake hot spots does not have to be a difficult process. Having a detailed lake map can reduce the amount of time it takes to find them. A certain amount of trial and error is involved in the process of determining which likely spots are producers and which are duds. But that is part of the challenge that makes this sport appealing.

How to Use This Guide

The information in this book is presented regionally, reflecting the differences in climate, terrain, and hydrology that define Texas fishing. Those regional zones are defined as Panhandle Plains, Prairies and Lakes, Piney Woods, Gulf Coast, South Texas Plains, Hill Country, and Big Bend. Fishing sites are numbered and placed on the accompanying maps to help anglers locate them geographically. Information on each site is presented in the following fashion:

- **Description of area:** Important features and conditions relevant to each site are detailed here.
- **Major species:** The important game species present at the site are listed here.
- **Rating of fishery:** The angling opportunities for each species are provided using four criteria: poor, fair, good, excellent.
- **The fishing:** The best angling opportunities for major gamefish species and when and where to pursue them are detailed here. Tips on what works best are included along with hot spot locations that reflect the seasonal nature of each resource.
- **Directions:** Details are provided on how to get there from the nearest town, city, or major landmark. Maps are included to provide a visual reference for locating each fishing site.
- **Additional information:** Special regulations, fees, and facilities for anglers, including boat ramps or marinas, and safety concerns are listed here.
- **Contact:** Names and numbers for relevant agencies involved in management or regulation of the resource and local services are provided here.

Prairies and Lakes Region

1 Lake Athens

Description of area: Lake Athens is a small but picturesque community water-supply lake located on Flat Creek, 4 miles southeast of the city of Athens. Surface area is approximately 1,700 acres and maximum depth is 50 feet. Water clarity is considered moderately clear.

Major species: Largemouth bass, crappie, sunfish, white bass, catfish

Rating of fishery: Largemouth bass fishing is excellent. Crappie and sunfish are good. White bass and catfish are fair.

The fishing: Lake Athens is noted for its largemouth bass fishery. Catches of 2- to 8-pound bass are common, with the occasional catch of a fish weighing 10 pounds or more reported. Plastic worms, shad-colored jerk baits, and spinner baits are among the most productive lures. The shoreline contains modest amounts of aquatic vegetation primarily on the northern end of the lake. There are numerous boat docks that provide ideal cover for bass. Riprap areas along the dam are another choice location. Best fishing seasons are spring and fall when bass are relating to shallow water habitats. The lake is also popular among anglers wanting to catch large sunfish

Lake Athens is small but scenic, containing excellent populations of many gamefish species.

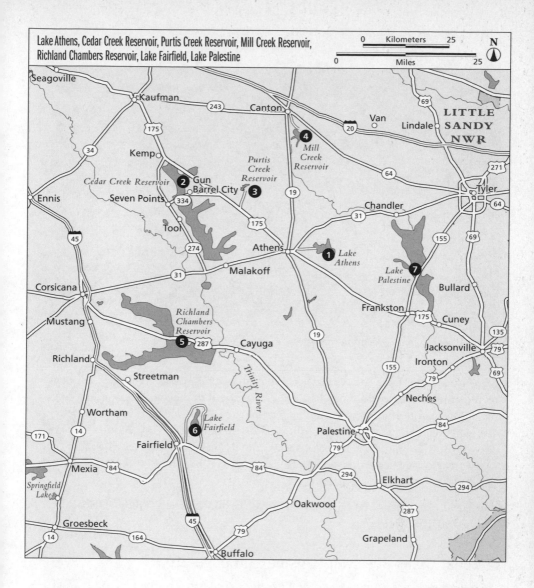

Lake Athens, Cedar Creek Reservoir, Purtis Creek Reservoir, Mill Creek Reservoir, Richland Chambers Reservoir, Lake Fairfield, Lake Palestine

on ultra-light tackle or a fly rod. The moderately clear water offers sight-fishing opportunities for sunfish when they are spawning in late spring and early summer. Sunfish up to 10 inches in length are not uncommon in Lake Athens. Crappie, white bass, and catfish opportunities are best during early spring and summer.

Directions: From Athens, travel southeast on FM 2495 approximately 4 miles and turn right on Marina Road just after crossing the bridge.

Map: DeLorme: Texas Atlas and Gazetteer: Page 47 K10

Additional information: There is a 2-lane launch ramp maintained by the city of Athens, and launching is free. The ramp is located on the eastern side of the lake

Lake Athens is small but scenic and provides excellent bass fishing opportunities.

on Marina Road. Lake Athens Cafe, Marina, and Campground are located adjacent to the ramp. Because of its small size, the lake does not receive excessive amounts of recreational traffic except on summer weekends. The fishery is managed under statewide regulations with the exception of largemouth bass. Largemouth bass are subject to a slot limit. Bass 14 inches or less and 21 inches or more may be retained. Only 1 bass 21 inches or longer may be kept per day. Bag limit is 5 bass per angler per day.

Contact: Lake Athens Marina, (903) 677-7490; Texas Parks and Wildlife District 3C Office, (903) 566-2161

2 Cedar Creek Reservoir (see map on page 25)

Description of area: Impounded in 1965 as a regional water-supply and flood-control reservoir on Kings Creek and Cedar Creek in western Henderson County, Cedar Creek Reservoir sprawls across more than 32,000 surface acres. The lake has multiple large and small coves and intermittent creeks drain into it. Much of the watershed area is composed of blackland clay soils. As a result, the upper section above the SH 334 Bridge is fairly shallow and remains turbid during most of the year. There is a moderate amount of standing flooded timber in this section. The lower third of the lake remains moderately clear. Maximum lake depth is 53 feet. The lake shoreline is highly developed.

Note: Due to drought, water levels at press time are low, resulting in many boat ramps being closed to the public. Check with local authorities before going.

Major species: Largemouth bass, crappie, blue and channel catfish, white bass, hybrid striped bass

Rating of fishery: Channel catfish and largemouth bass fishing are good. Crappie, blue catfish, white bass, and hybrid striped bass are excellent.

The fishing: The best area of the lake to fish for largemouth bass is the lower third, where the water remains moderately clear year-round. Native vegetation is sparse and most of the bass will be found around the plentiful boat docks surrounding the shoreline. "Shooting the docks" is the phrase most bass anglers use to describe the technique necessary to lure bass into striking. Lures are cast under the docks with a sidearm motion, allowed to sink, and then retrieved out to deeper water. Jigs, soft-plastic creature baits, and jerk baits are all productive lures for this type of structure fishing. In the spring bass will move to shallow coves and adjacent flats, where they are susceptible to a wide variety of lures, to spawn.

During the summer they will move to boat docks and other deep-water structure along creek channels. In the fall bass will follow forage species into the creeks as water temperatures cool. Shad-colored crankbaits are a good choice to catch them. Crappie fishermen concentrate on boat docks, bridge pilings, and brush piles to catch limits of large crappie on Cedar Creek. The lake has an excellent population of these popular species and hundreds of brush piles and docks in which to look for them.

White bass and hybrid striper fishing at this lake are exceptional during the summer months. Large schools of both species can be found in open water areas

Big hybrid striped bass like this one are common in Cedar Creek Lake.

relating to drop-offs around islands and main lake points. They will push schools of shad to the surface and feed on them in a frenzy of activity. Just about any lure that mimics the size and color of the forage fish will be struck. When they are not feeding on the surface, small slabs or spoons in chrome, white, or chartreuse colors jigged vertically over a suspended school will usually produce strikes.

Cedar Creek is also known as a highly productive catfishing destination. Blue catfish can easily be caught on cut bait all over the lake. The upper end of the reservoir is the best area. Find a timbered creek channel and fish the edges and adjacent flats with cut shad suspended under a float for bait.

Directions: Cedar Creek Reservoir is located 45 miles southeast of Dallas on US 175. At Kemp, exit SH 274 and turn right. Continue approximately 10 miles to SH 334 and turn left.

Map: DeLorme: Texas Atlas and Gazetteer: Page 47 J, K7

Additional information: There are 10 public access points with launch ramps on Cedar Creek. Two are free ramps and the other 8 are operated by private concessionaires that charge a small fee to launch. Chamber Island just off the SH 334 Bridge between Seven Points and Gun Barrel City has a no-fee public ramp. The free Caney Cove ramp is located just south of Caney City on SH 198. The ramp is on the northeast side of the bridge crossing the cove. Abundant campgrounds and cabins for rent are scattered around the lake. Contact the Greater Cedar Creek Chamber of Commerce for a listing of available lodging. The fishery is managed by statewide rules and regulations with no special exemptions.

Contact: Greater Cedar Creek Chamber of Commerce, (903) 887-3152; Texas Parks and Wildlife District Office, (903) 566-2161

3 Purtis Creek Reservoir (see map on page 25)

Description of area: The 349-acre reservoir is part of Purtis Creek State Park, operated by Texas Parks and Wildlife on FM 316 just north of the city of Eustace. The lake was designed specifically for fishing and opened to the public in 1988. Most of the timber and natural features of the basin were left intact during construction to provide excellent habitat for the fishery to follow. The maximum depth is 30 feet and the water is moderately clear most of the year. Bank-fishing access is very good and a limited number of boats are allowed daily. Outboard motor use is limited to idling only. The lake has a plentiful supply of native aquatic vegetation. Two fishing piers are available for anglers to use.

Major species: Largemouth bass, crappie, channel catfish, sunfish

Rating of fishery: Largemouth bass fishing is excellent; crappie, catfish, and sunfish are very good.

The fishing: Purtis Creek Reservoir was designed and constructed as a trophy fishing lake for largemouth bass. Special catch-and-release regulations have been in place since the fishery was founded in the 1980s. The lake is well known for produc-

Largemouth bass fishing is catch-and-release only at Purtis Creek.

ing large bass, and 3 fish weighing more than 13 pounds have been donated to the ShareLunker Program. Live bait fishing for bass is popular on this state park lake. Late winter to early spring is when most anglers target this small, quality fishery, coinciding with spawning season. The large bass move to shallow areas to reproduce, becoming more accessible to anglers.

Somewhat unusual is that many of the large bass Purtis is known for have been caught while fishing from a pier in late summer using live goldfish for bait. Purtis is also known as a producer of large sunfish. The state record bluegill was caught from this lake and it weighed a whopping 1.81 pounds. Channel catfish are stocked annually, making this lake popular with bank-fishing campers. Crappie fishermen also do well due to the large amount of woody cover available.

Directions: Purtis Creek Reservoir is located 65 miles southeast of Dallas. Travel US 175 to Eustace and then turn north on FM 316. Drive 3.5 miles to the park entrance on the left side of the road.

Map: DeLorme: Texas Atlas and Gazetteer: Page 47 J8

Additional information: Fishing in Purtis is limited to rod and reel only. The lake has special regulations for largemouth bass. All bass must be released immediately except fish over 21 inches in length, which may be put in a live well and transported

Lighted fishing piers at Purtis Creek provide good angling opportunities for shoreline anglers.

to a lakeside weigh station, weighed, and then released unless it qualifies for the ShareLunker Program. The daily limit for blue and channel catfish in any combination is 5 per person with no minimum length requirement. Other species are governed by statewide regulations. The park rents canoes and kayaks. There is a small per-person day-use entrance fee.

Contact: Purtis Creek State Park, (903) 425-2332

4 Mill Creek Reservoir (see map on page 25)

Description of area: Mill Creek Reservoir is a small water-supply reservoir controlled by the city of Canton. Surface area encompasses 237 acres and the lake is moderately clear most of the year. The lake is located on a tributary of the Sabine River, with fairly constant water levels and a maximum depth of 25 feet. Aquatic vegetation is sparse with some flooded timber available. The shoreline is irregular with many small coves and inlets.

Major species: Largemouth bass, black and white crappie, catfish, sunfish

Rating of fishery: Largemouth bass fishing is good, crappie is good, catfish and sunfish are fair to poor.

The fishing: Mill Creek Reservoir is noted for producing catches of trophy-sized largemouth bass. The lake record for the species is over 14 pounds and the lake regularly produces quality-size bass for anglers who fish it. Early spring is the most productive time of the year to fish for the large bass this lake produces. Bass move shallow to spawn along the shorelines, allowing anglers a better opportunity to sight-fish for them when they are on their nest. Soft-plastic creature baits and jigs account for a majority of the large bass caught from this lake. The lake is not well known except among local anglers, and it is a sleeper for producing trophy-sized largemouth bass. In 2005 the lake was stocked by the Texas Parks and Wildlife Department with 6,000 fingerlings spawned from female ShareLunker bass that weighed more than 13 pounds. The lake is also a popular site for fly fishermen who target sunfish species with a fly rod.

Directions: Mill Creek Reservoir is located just southeast of Canton off SH 243 between SH 19 and SH 64. Travel east on SH 243 and turn right on Arnold Paul Road. Follow road to the launch ramp.

Map: DeLorme: Texas Atlas and Gazetteer: Page 47 I9

Additional information: A boat launch permit is required by the city of Canton. There is 1 single-lane concrete boat ramp, and the parking lot will hold a maximum of 50 vehicles. A courtesy dock and 2 fishing piers are available. The area is open all year. Statewide regulations for fishing apply with the exception of largemouth bass. A 14- to 21-inch slot limit is in effect for Mill Creek. Bass 14 inches or less or 21 inches or greater may be retained up to 5 fish per person per day. Only 1 bass 21 inches or larger may be kept each day. Local camping and lodging information is available from the Canton Chamber of Commerce.

Contact: City of Canton, (903) 567-2826; Texas Parks and Wildlife District Office, (903) 593-5077; Canton Chamber of Commerce, (903) 567-2991

5 Richland Chambers Reservoir (see map on page 25)

Description of area: This giant reservoir sprawls across approximately 44,000 surface acres and is the fourth-largest body of water in the state. Its 2 main tributaries are Richland Creek to the west and Chambers Creek, from which the reservoir gets its name, to the east. The watershed area is primarily woodland and agricultural lands. The large amount of sediment washed into the lake during inclement weather keeps it slightly turbid on the upper ends in winter and spring. This has a tendency to limit the amount of aquatic vegetation present. Large tracts of timber in the main creek arms were left for fish habitat during construction. The lake shoreline is still relatively undeveloped. Maximum depth is 75 feet and the area below the US 287 Bridge remains moderately clear most of the year. This lake receives little relative fishing pressure because of its size and distance from major urban centers.

Major species: White bass, hybrid striped bass, white and black crappie, largemouth bass, blue and channel catfish

Rating of fishery: Fishing for white bass, hybrid stripers, catfish, and crappie is excellent. Largemouth bass fishing is fair to good.

The fishing: The lack of abundant aquatic plants and the turbid nature of shallow water areas on this reservoir limit the quantity but not quality of the bass fishing.

Richland Chambers is noted for producing trophy-sized hybrid striped bass.

The lake has been heavily stocked with largemouth bass since it was impounded in 1988, and efforts to enhance the amount of vegetation in the coves and shoreline areas are helping the bass fishery become more productive.

Plastic worms, spinner baits, and crankbaits are the most consistent bite producers. Most successful bass fishermen concentrate on the many timbered creek channels and adjacent flats in clear-water areas to find willing fish. White-bass and hybrid-striper anglers usually have no problem finding acres of hungry fish on Richland. These fish are abundant and readily take small shad-imitating lures. During the spring, summer, and fall, they feed on the surface early in the morning and late in the evening. This behavior presents some of the most exciting top-water lure action possible. When they are not active on top, they will suspend in large schools over humps and along creek channels in the lower end of the reservoir. A slab or spoon jigged up through them vertically is all it usually takes to get them to strike. Trolling lures are also a popular option for these hard-fighting and table-tasty fish.

Richland Chambers is also known for its excellent crappie fishing. Just about any creek channel with standing timber will be holding large numbers of fish. The pilings on the US 287 Bridge and the FM 2859 Bridge are also prime locations to catch a mess of crappie. Minnows and small jigs are the favored baits. Catfish are abundant all over the lake and will readily bite on cut bait or prepared baits. Wintertime fishing for large blue catfish using cut bait is also a popular angling activity. ***Directions:*** Richland Chambers Reservoir lies just southeast of Corsicana between SH 31 and FM 416. The easiest access is US 287, which crosses the lake at its middle.

Map: *DeLorme: Texas Atlas and Gazetteer:* Page 59 B7

Additional information: The fishery is managed under statewide regulations except for blue catfish, which are subject to a 30- to 45-inch slot limit. Blue catfish 30 inches and less or 45 inches and longer may be retained, with a limit of 1 per day that measures 45 inches or longer. Otherwise, the daily bag limit is 25 blue and channel catfish combined. Multiple free ramps and private launch sites are available around the lake. Lodging sites and restaurants are numerous. Contact the Corsicana Chamber of Commerce for a list.

Contact: Corsicana Chamber of Commerce, (903) 874-4731; Texas Parks and Wildlife District Office, (903) 566-2161

6 Lake Fairfield (see map on page 25)

Description of area: Fairfield is a small, power-plant-cooling reservoir located just northeast of the city of Fairfield. Surface area is 2,159 acres and maximum depth is 49 feet at the dam. The surrounding terrain consists of oak woods and grasslands. The reservoir was impounded in 1969 as a cooling basin for electric power production. The lake and its southern and eastern shorelines are part of Fairfield State Park, operated by the Texas Parks and Wildlife Department. Water levels fluctuate up to 4 feet in normal rainfall years and the water remains moderately clear. Population in this predominately agricultural area is sparse, yet access to this popular fishery is easy via I-45, which passes on the outskirts of Fairfield.

Major species: Largemouth bass, red drum, catfish

Rating of fishery: Fishing for largemouth bass, red drum, and catfish is excellent.

The fishing: Lake Fairfield provides anglers with an opportunity for year-round warmwater fishing because of its use by Texas Utilities as an electric-power-plant-cooling reservoir. Another unique aspect of the fishery is the presence of red drum.

Red drum are an important gamefish in Texas coastal bays and have the ability to survive in a freshwater environment with adequate mineral content and warm water. This adaptation allows them to thrive in selected habitats inland. They exist as a put-and-take fishery as they cannot reproduce in freshwater. Fishery crews stocked Fairfield with 327,000 red drum fingerlings in 2011. The lake and state record red drum was caught at Fairfield and weighed 36.8 pounds.

Most anglers target them by trolling large crankbaits or using live or cut bait. Fairfield has been stocked with plant-eating tilapia in an effort to manage the abundant aquatic vegetation present due to the year-round warmth of the water. Many anglers catch small tilapia with a cast net and use them as bait for red drum. Threadfin shad or bluegills also work well.

The warmwater environment is also a boon to largemouth bass fishing. The fishing is especially good in winter as the bass remain active and will spawn earlier in the season than normal. This factor makes Fairfield a choice location for anglers wanting to experience springtime bass-fishing conditions when non-heated lakes are still in the grip of winter temperatures. The abundant shoreline vegetation is where most of the action takes place. Soft-plastic worms, spinner baits, and jigs are

Lake Fairfield is a power plant lake and is heavily stocked annually with redfish that grow to more than 20 pounds.

the lures of choice. The lake record for largemouth bass is 13.01 pounds. Fishing for catfish using cut and prepared baits is also popular on this small but productive lake.

Note: Lake Fairfield experienced back-to-back major fish kills in 2010 and 2011. As of press time, Texas Parks and Wildlife suspended stocking of the lake until further notice. Contact the TPWD District Office for current information.

Directions: From Fairfield travel on FM 2570 for 6 miles to FM 3285, turn right, and follow the road to the park entrance. The lake lies 90 miles south of Dallas and 150 miles north of Houston.

Map: *DeLorme: Texas Atlas and Gazetteer:* Page 59 D8

Additional information: Day use of the lake and park is subject to a per-person fee. Facilities available include 2 boat ramps, courtesy docks, fish-cleaning stations, campgrounds with electricity and water, and a lighted fishing pier. Fishing is subject to statewide regulations with 2 exceptions. The minimum length limit for largemouth bass is 18 inches. Daily bag limit is 5 bass per angler per day. For red drum, the minimum length limit is 20 inches with no maximum size restriction. Bag limit is 3 fish per person per day. Contact the Fairfield Chamber of Commerce for a list of local lodges and eateries.

Contact: Fairfield Lake State Park, (903) 389-4514; Texas Parks and Wildlife District Office, (903) 566-2161; Fairfield Chamber of Commerce, (903) 389-5792

7 Lake Palestine (see map on page 25)

Description of area: Lake Palestine is located on the Neches River 15 miles southwest of Tyler. Surface area is 25,500 acres and the maximum depth is 58 feet. Kickapoo Creek is the other main tributary to this popular East Texas fishery. The shoreline area of the lake is heavily developed except for the northern end, where the major tributaries enter the lake. Aquatic vegetation and standing timber are abundant in the main creek channels. Patches of timber also provide habitat in the main lake north of the SH 155 Bridge. The water remains moderately clear during the summer and fall.

Note: Due to drought, water levels at press time are low at many of the ramps. Before visiting, contact local authorities for information on the best way to access the lake.

Major species: White bass, hybrid striped bass, largemouth bass, black and white crappie, and blue, channel, and flathead catfish

Rating of fishery: Fishing for white bass, hybrid striped bass, and all catfish species is excellent. Largemouth bass and crappie are good.

The fishing: Palestine offers anglers a smorgasbord of fishing opportunities. Largemouth bass anglers typically do best on the upper half of the lake in the spring, when bass move shallow to spawn in the creeks. Popular spots are Kickapoo Creek, Flat Creek, Cobb Creek, and Saline Bay. Spinner baits, jigs, and crankbaits in shad patterns are favorite producers. In the summer and fall, fishing around the bridges and the dam area produces well. In late winter to early spring, white bass run up Kickapoo Creek and the Neches River, providing excellent fishing for these sporty and tasty gamefish on light tackle.

The river and creek are accessible for several miles above the lake to small flat-bottomed boats when flow conditions are optimal. Limits of white bass are typical during their migration. Small jigs and spinners account for most of the fish caught when they are in the tributaries. Crappie anglers also do well on Palestine. Abundant brush piles have been placed for habitat from the SH 155 Bridge to the dam. The timber just above the bridge and the bridge pilings are also excellent locations to catch crappie on Palestine.

The area of the lake below the 155 Bridge to the dam is hybrid-striper country. Successful angling techniques include trolling shad-imitating crankbaits and vertical slab fishing along the river channel, bridge pilings, and the ends of main lake points. In the summer top-water action early and late in the day is a regular pattern. Catfishing is excellent on the flats from Flat Creek to the 155 Bridge using live and cut bait. The state record for flathead catfish on rod and reel came from Lake Palestine. It was caught on live bait and weighed 98.5 pounds.

Directions: From Tyler travel southwest on SH 155 for 15 miles. The lake is bordered on the north by SH 31 and on the south by US 175. There are multiple lake access roads from each of those highways.

Map: DeLorme: Texas Atlas and Gazetteer: Page 59 A11

The annual white bass run up tributaries on Lake Palestine provides excellent fishing for these feisty gamefish.

Additional information: Public access to Palestine consists of 5 free major ramps with adequate parking and a dozen or more private ramps that charge a small fee. Facilities available at private sites include motels, camping, cabins, fish-cleaning stations, and marinas. Contact the Tyler Convention & Visitors Bureau for a complete list of area businesses that cater to fishermen. The fishery is managed by statewide regulations, with no special provisions.

Contact: Tyler Convention & Visitors Bureau, (800) 235-5712; Texas Parks and Wildlife District Office, (903) 566-2161

8 Lake Tawakoni

Description of area: Lake Tawakoni sprawls across 3 northeast Texas counties 15 miles southeast of Greenville. Surface area of the lake is 38,000 acres and maximum depth is 70 feet. The lake is bounded on the north by US 69 and by US 80 on the south. The shoreline area is heavily developed on the north end above the Two-Mile Bridge connecting the community of East Tawakoni and the city of Quinlan to the west. The Tawakoni watershed is mostly composed of agricultural grasslands and mixed hardwood areas on a black clay soil. After periods of heavy rainfall, the upper half of the lake can become quite turbid. The lower half of the lake remains slightly stained year-round. Various patches of standing timber remain in the lake, and aquatic vegetation is limited to the backs of major creeks. The shoreline is irregular with 2 major bays and many small inlets feeding into the main reservoir. The major tributaries are Caddo Creek and 2 forks of the Sabine River.

Docks provide good shoreline cover on Lake Tawakoni.

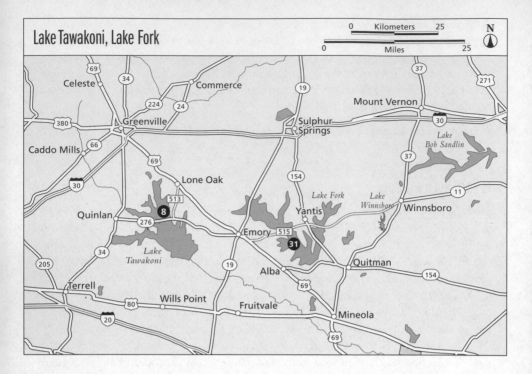

Lake Tawakoni, Lake Fork

Major species: White bass, hybrid striped bass, striped bass, largemouth bass, crappie, and channel, blue, and flathead catfish

Rating of fishery: White, hybrid, and striped bass and catfish are excellent. Crappie fishing is fair.

The fishing: Tawakoni is noted for being one of the top white, hybrid, and striped bass lakes in Texas. The lake is stocked heavily with hybrids and stripers annually. The fishing for these 3 species is a year-round business on Tawakoni. During the spring, summer, and fall, anglers delight in catching them on top-water lures when they push schools of shad to the surface and feed on them. Small shad-imitating top-water lures and slabs in white, chrome, or chartreuse are the lures favored by most anglers. When they are not feeding on the surface, jigging a slab over deep-water structure is usually productive. Larger lures in the same patterns will entice the hybrids and stripers.

Live shad fishing is also popular for these fish. The lake record for hybrid stripers is just over 15 pounds and for striped bass, 22 pounds. Many anglers also troll for them around main lake points and the numerous underwater humps located in the south end of the reservoir. Largemouth bass fishing is good in the creeks and coves with adequate habitat. Lack of aquatic vegetation on the main lake is the main limiting factor. Spring spawning season is the best time to tangle with largemouth bass. They move to shallow cover along shorelines and defend their nests aggressively. In the summer and fall, they will school in the mouths of major coves and along deep-water creeks with flooded timber. During this period they become particularly susceptible to small crankbaits in shad patterns. Tawakoni is also a premium destination to catch catfish. The lake abounds with a healthy population of channel, blue, and flatheads. Drifting cut or live bait across points and underwater islands will usually result in limits. Bank fishing with prepared baits is a good way to catch them too. Another popular technique is fishing live crickets under a cork along the dam face in early summer.

Directions: From Greenville take US 69 southeast for 15 miles to Lone Oak. Turn right on FM 513 and continue to SH 276, which crosses the lake from the east side. Or take SH 34 from Greenville south to Quinlan and turn left on SH 276.

Map: DeLorme: Texas Atlas and Gazetteer: Page 47 F8

Additional information: The fishery is managed under statewide regulations with no special exemptions. Access to the lake is well developed, with 5 public ramps and a wide variety of private facilities available. These include marinas, campgrounds, bait-and-tackle shops, and motels. Contact the Greenville Chamber Convention & Visitors Bureau for a list of facilities in the area. Lake Tawakoni State Park, operated by the Texas Parks and Wildlife Department, is located on the western shore in the main lake area. From Wills Point, travel north on SH 47 to FM 2475, turn left (east), and continue for 4 miles to the park entrance. Contact the park for reservation information.

Contact: Greenville Chamber Convention & Visitors Bureau, (903) 455-1510; Texas Parks and Wildlife District Office, (903) 593-5077; Lake Tawakoni State Park, (903) 560-7123

The spillway at Lake Tawakoni is an excellent place to catch various species of gamefish.

9 Lake Ray Hubbard

Description of area: This reservoir is located on the east fork of the Trinity River and is surrounded by urban areas of the Dallas Metroplex. Surface area is 22,750 acres and maximum depth is 40 feet. The watershed for this area is typical of the blackland prairie region of north-central Texas and as a result the lake remains somewhat turbid most of the year. The lower end below the I-30 Bridge gets moderately clear in late summer. Scattered pockets of standing timber exist above the I-30 Bridge, and the riverbanks of the Trinity River feeding the lake are vegetated. Scattered areas of hydrilla on shallow flats provide habitat for largemouth bass. Some submerged vegetation is present in the backs of coves.

Major species: White bass, hybrid striped bass, largemouth bass, channel catfish, blue catfish, white crappie

Rating of fishery: Fishing for largemouth bass and crappie is good. White bass, hybrid striped bass, and catfish are excellent.

The fishing: Lake Ray Hubbard is noted for its excellent populations of white bass, hybrid stripers, and catfish. The best fishing area for whites and hybrids lies east of the I-30 Bridge. Hot spots include the Robertson Park Flats, the power plant discharge area, the dam face, and the mouth of Yankee and Rush Creek. Top-water action is possible daily during the warm months and anglers have good success using small top waters, slabs, spoons, and crankbaits in shad patterns.

Largemouth bass anglers do well fishing the mouth and banks of the Trinity River, the riprap areas along the SH 66 Bridge, the humps around the power

Blue catfish like this one are common in Lake Ray Hubbard.

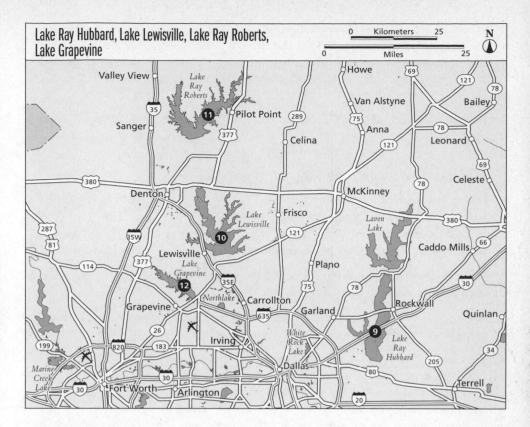

plant discharge, and Yankee and Rush Creek on the northeast end of the lake and the rocks along the dam. Small shallow-running shad-colored crankbaits, lipless crankbaits in black or blue and chrome, and soft-plastic drop-shot rigs in pumpkin colors are excellent lure choices. Crappie fishermen target the bridge pilings and the adjacent rock-lined abutments as well as the standing timber on the upper lake in the spring. Numerous brush piles are located at the mouths of coves on the lower end of the lake and near the dam. Catfish anglers have great success drifting cut bait across the shallow flats and using prepared baits under a float along the bridge abutment rocks and the dam face.

Directions: From Dallas take I-30 north 17 miles to the city of Garland and take the Dalrock exit to Robertson Park.

Map: DeLorme: Texas Atlas and Gazetteer: Page 46 F5

Additional information: Despite its urban location and easy access, Ray Hubbard is a very productive fishery. The lake is heavily stocked annually by TPWD to maintain catch rates at optimum levels. Since 2001 more than 1.5 million largemouth bass and 2.13 million hybrid stripers have been stocked in the lake. The lake record for largemouth bass was set in 2002 with a fish that weighed just over 14 pounds. The state record hybrid striper was caught from Ray Hubbard too. It weighed 19.66 pounds. Multiple free ramps are available on access roads from I-30 and SH 66. The fishery is managed under statewide regulations. There are no special regulations. The shoreline is heavily developed and there is no camping available around the lakeshore. Robertson Park is a large day-use facility with multiple boat ramps and bank-fishing sites. Other services of interest to anglers are available nearby. Contact the city of Garland for a list.

Contact: City of Garland, (972) 205-2000; Texas Parks and Wildlife District Office, (817) 732-0761

10 Lake Lewisville (see map on page 41)

Description of area: Located on the Elm Fork of the Trinity River northwest of Dallas. Surface area is 29,500 acres and maximum depth is 67 feet. Lake levels can fluctuate as much as 4 to 10 feet annually and the water clarity is usually stained. Shorelines are heavily developed except for Corps of Engineers parklands.

Major species: Largemouth bass, spotted bass, white bass, hybrid striped bass, white crappie, channel and blue catfish

Rating of fishery: Catfish, crappie, and white bass are excellent; largemouth bass, hybrid striper, and spotted bass are very good.

The fishing: Lake Lewisville is noted for its excellent white bass, crappie, and catfishing opportunities, but its reputation as a largemouth bass hot spot has been kept relatively quiet. The lake has been heavily stocked for the past 10 years with largemouth bass, and those efforts are paying off. Bass fishing on Lewisville has become good enough to attract major bass tournaments. The lake has substantial stump fields, standing timber, rocky shorelines, coves, and brush pockets along with numerous man-made structures along the shoreline that provide excellent habitat for bass. Soft-plastic worms and spinner baits are effective in the spring; crankbaits, jigs, and jerk baits work best in summer and fall. Crappie anglers do well on minnows and jigs around the bridges and in the many timbered creek channels. White bass and hybrids are most plentiful around main lake points in the Park Cove and Sand Bass Cut areas. Catfish anglers do very well around the 121 Cut riprap along the I-35E Bridge and points west of the dam on cut bait and live bait. Spotted bass anglers target riprap areas, rocky shorelines, and deep-water rock piles. Small crankbaits and jigs in crawfish patterns are the most effective lures.

Directions: From Dallas travel north on I-35E approximately 25 miles. The I-35E Bridge crosses the Hickory Creek arm of the lake on the west side of the reservoir.

Map: DeLorme: Texas Atlas and Gazetteer: Page 46 C3

Additional information: The Army Corps of Engineers is the controlling authority on Lewisville and maintains and operates numerous parks around the perimeter. Contact them for a list of parks and amenities offered. They also have a free lake map available upon request. Many other public access points and businesses catering to angler needs are located around the lake. Contact the city of Lewisville for lodging and other angler-related services. Lewisville is heavily used by the public for water-based recreation on weekends. The best fishing opportunities occur during the week in spring and fall. Lake records for largemouth bass, hybrid striped bass, and spotted bass have all been broken since 2005, which is another testimonial to the quality fishing this lake offers anglers.

The fishery is managed under statewide regulations except for blue catfish, which are subject to a 30- to 45-inch slot limit. Blue catfish 30 inches and less or 45 inches and longer may be retained, with a limit of 1 per day that measures 45 inches or longer. Otherwise, the daily bag limit is 25 blue and channel catfish combined.

Contact: US Army Corps of Engineers, (469) 645-9100; Texas Parks and Wildlife District Office, (817) 732-0761; city of Lewisville (972) 219-3400

11 Lake Ray Roberts (see map on page 41)

Description of area: This large impoundment is located on the Elm Fork of the Trinity River near the north Texas city of Denton. The lake encompasses 29,000 surface acres with a maximum depth of 100 feet at the dam. Water fluctuations in a normal rainfall year are 3 to 5 feet and the water clarity is usually clear. Several thousand acres of standing timber were left in the many small and large creek channels, and aquatic vegetation is abundant around the lake. Ray Roberts has been described as one of the most habitat-rich reservoirs in Texas.

Major species: Largemouth bass, white bass, crappie, catfish, sunfish

Rating of fishery: Largemouth bass, crappie, and white bass are excellent. Catfish is very good.

A typical cove on Lake Ray Roberts draws anglers to this highly productive bass fishery.

The fishing: This sprawling impoundment was constructed not only as a water-supply reservoir but also to provide excellent habitat for recreational fishing. Acres of standing timber, multiple creek channels, flooded pond dams, submerged road beds, stump fields, and thousands of acres of native aquatic vegetation as well as dozens of submerged brush piles make this lake a fisherman's dream. Bass fishing is superb in the spring during spawning season in shallow areas along the extensive shoreline. White spinner baits and pearl flukes are top choices for largemouth bass when they are nesting. Most trophy bass are caught on dark-colored jigs in the late winter months before moving to spawning areas.

During the summer fish the flooded timber with Carolina-rigged soft plastics or deep-running crankbaits. In the fall jerk baits and spinner baits are top producers in the mouths of coves and in creek channels. Crappie anglers do best in early spring along the brushy shorelines with jigs and minnows. During the hot months fish the creek channels with flooded timber in 20 to 30 feet of water. In the winter, crappie school up on deep-water brush piles around Wolf Island. Slow-trolling small jigs or vertical jigging are the best techniques to catch them. Catfish anglers do well on live shiners, cut and prepared baits on the Ball Camp Flats, and along the dam during the warm months.

Directions: From Denton travel east on US 380 7 miles to US 377. Turn north and travel approximately 15 miles to Pilot Point.

Map: DeLorme: Texas Atlas and Gazetteer: Page 46 B2

Additional information: Texas Parks and Wildlife operates Lake Ray Roberts State Park, which includes 3 main units: Isle du Bois, Johnson Branch, and the Jordan. The Jordan Park Unit includes Lantana Lodge, which is a full-service facility featuring fine dining and excellent lodging. Contact each unit for details on fees and facilities available. The fishery is managed under statewide regulations with the following exceptions: Largemouth bass 14 inches and less or 24 inches or longer may be retained. The limit is 5 fish per angler per day. Only 1 fish 24 inches or longer may be kept daily. Contact the city of Pilot Point for a list of angler-related services available around the lake.

Contact: City of Pilot Point, (817) 686-5385; Ray Roberts State Park, Isle du Bois Unit, (940) 686-2148, Johnson Branch Unit, (940) 637-2294, Jordan Unit, (940) 686-0261; Texas Parks and Wildlife Department District Fisheries Office, (903) 786-2389

12 Lake Grapevine (see map on page 41)

Description of area: Grapevine is located just north of the city of Grapevine, 20 miles northwest of Dallas, and covers 6,900 surface acres. Situated on Denton Creek, a tributary of the Trinity River, the water remains moderately stained year-round. Maximum depth is 65 feet. The shoreline has numerous rocky areas. The lake is surrounded by residential development. Water levels fluctuate 5 to 10 feet annually. The Army Corps of Engineers is the controlling water authority.

Major species: Largemouth bass, spotted bass, white bass, white crappie, blue and channel catfish

Rating of fishery: Largemouth bass and white bass fishing is excellent. White crappie, spotted bass, and catfish are good.

The fishing: Largemouth bass and white bass are the 2 species that draw most anglers to Grapevine. This small lake is full of fish-attracting structure including rock piles, drop-offs, ledges, and coves full of standing timber. Bass anglers target the shorelines with plastic worms, jigs, and crankbaits in crawfish and shad patterns in the spring. In the warm months grubs and deep-diving crankbaits work well on the ledges and rock piles. Spotted bass populations are good in Grapevine, and they can be caught on the same lures used for largemouth but need to be in smaller sizes. Spotted bass like to live in the rocky areas, and using lures that resemble 2- to 3-inch crawfish are a sure means to attract them. White bass anglers can find large schools of these feisty fish around the main lake points and adjacent flats on the lower end of the lake and near the dam. Small top waters, spoons, and slabs that imitate shad are the most productive lures. Look for crappie in the timbered coves in the Twin Coves area and under the numerous boathouses scattered around the lake. Catfish anglers will find good fishing using cut bait, stink bait, and shrimp along the dam area, Rockledge Park, and Meadowmere Park flats.

Directions: From Grapevine take SH 114 (Northwest Highway) to Dove Road to Dove Loop North approximately 2 miles and then to Oak Grove Park.

Map: DeLorme: Texas Atlas and Gazetteer: Page 46 D2

Additional information: Facilities around the lake are managed by the Army Corps of Engineers and various municipalities. A free lake map is available from the Corps of Engineers. Two parks offer overnight camping: Silver Lake and Twin Coves. The fishery is managed under statewide regulations with the exception of largemouth bass, for which there is a 14- to 18-inch slot limit. Bass 14 inches and less in length or 18 inches or more may be retained. Daily bag limit of all species of black bass in any combination is 5 per angler.

Contact: US Army Corps of Engineers, (817) 865-2600; Texas Parks and Wildlife District Office, (817) 732-0761; Twin Coves Park, (972) 539-1030; Silver Lake Park (817) 329-8993

13 Eagle Mountain Lake

Description of area: Eagle Mountain lies a few miles north of the city of Lake Worth on the west fork of the Trinity River. The lake surface area is 8,738 acres and maximum depth is 47 feet. Water clarity is normally clear in the lower end of the reservoir and somewhat stained in the upper end. Vegetation is scarce, but on the upper end there are reed beds that provide habitat. The shoreline is rocky and has numerous boathouses in the lower sections of the reservoir that attract and hold gamefish. Lake levels fluctuate between 2 and 9 feet annually.

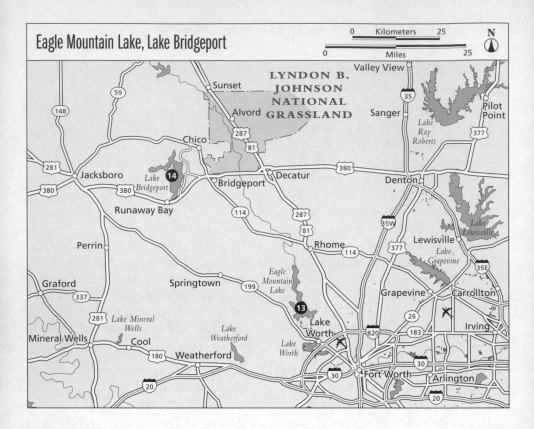

Eagle Mountain Lake, Lake Bridgeport

Major species: Largemouth bass, spotted bass, smallmouth bass, white crappie, blue and channel catfish, white bass

Rating of fishery: Crappie and white bass fishing is excellent. Largemouth bass, spotted bass, smallmouth bass, and catfish are good.

The fishing: Largemouth bass fishing is the primary draw to Eagle Mountain Lake. State fishery crews have heavily stocked the lake with Florida-strain largemouth bass since 1988 and the effort has paid off. Even though a lack of vegetation around the shoreline limits the bass fishery somewhat, the bass have adapted to available rocky points and bluff structure and congregate around numerous boat docks and fishing piers that surround the shoreline. The rocky areas are also preferred habitat for the resident spotted and smallmouth bass. Crawfish-imitating jigs, plastic grubs, drop-shot rigs, and small-to-medium crankbaits are all productive patterns. Crappie fishermen concentrate on the boat docks and the rocky points on the south end of the lake. White bass fishing is excellent on the numerous points and ledges during the summer in the southern portions of the reservoir. Small top-water lures, slabs, and spoons in white, chrome, and chartreuse are angler favorites. Fishing for channel and blue catfish is productive on prepared and natural baits in the upper end of the reservoir and in the creek channels.

Directions: From the city of Lake Worth, drive northwest on TX 199 for 8 miles. Turn north on Boat Club Road and west on 10-Mile Bridge Road and follow to Twin Points Marina.

Map: DeLorme: Texas Atlas and Gazetteer: Page 45 E12

Additional information: Free maps of the lake are available from the Tarrant Regional Water District, which is the controlling authority for Eagle Mountain. The fishery is managed under statewide regulations. There is a free public ramp located at Shady Grove Park just north of the city of Azle. Other private facilities are available around the lake.

Contact: Tarrant Regional Water District, (817) 237-8585; city of Azle, (817) 444-2541; Texas Parks and Wildlife District Office, (817) 732-0761

14 Lake Bridgeport (see map on page 46)

Description of area: This 11,954-acre reservoir is located just west of the city of Bridgeport, on the west fork of the Trinity River, and spreads across Jack and Wise Counties in north-central Texas. The controlling water authority is the Tarrant Regional Water District in Fort Worth. The lake can fluctuate up to 12 feet annually in its capacity as a city water source. With over 170 miles of shoreline consisting of large areas of riprap, rocky shorelines, gravel pits, and many coves with irregular features, Bridgeport is full of fish-attracting structure. Water clarity is normally moderately clear year-round.

Major species: Largemouth bass, smallmouth bass, spotted bass, white and hybrid striped bass, crappie, catfish

Rating of fishery: Crappie and white and hybrid striped bass are excellent. Largemouth bass, smallmouth bass, spotted bass, and catfish are good.

The fishing: Bridgeport offers a wide variety of species for anglers to pursue. Black bass anglers concentrate on the shoreline areas and the rock piles to find fish willing to strike a wide variety of lures. Carolina-rigged plastic lizards, drop-shot rigs with finesse worms in natural colors, and shad-imitating crankbaits are good choices for largemouth, smallmouth, and spotted bass. The gravel piles around Windy Point and Steele Island are good locations for summertime action with jigs and spoons and Texas-rigged plastic worms.

White bass and hybrid striped bass move up and down the lake seasonally. In the spring they move to the mouths of tributaries and then into the creeks to spawn. During the summer and fall, they relocate to the deep-water areas near Rattlesnake Island, the gravel piles, the riprap along the dam, and at the ends of submerged main lake points. Small shad-imitating crankbaits, jigs, and spoons are a sure bet to entice them. Crappie fishing is best in the spring when they move to shoreline shallows to spawn and then again in winter when large schools congregate on deep-water structure. Minnows and jigs are the best bet to catch them. Fishing for catfish is very productive in spring when creeks bring copious quantities of food into the lake and the fish move to the flats at the mouths of the creeks to feed. During the summer they can be caught by drifting cut bait over the flats around Rattlesnake Island.

Directions: From the city of Bridgeport, drive west on US 380 approximately 5 miles and cross the bridge on the southern end of the lake. Turn right to Runaway Bay Marina on the first road after crossing the bridge. The ramp and marina are open year-round. A fee is required to launch.

Map: DeLorme: Texas Atlas and Gazetteer: Page 45 C10

Additional information: Wise County Park and Northside Marina offer the only camping facilities on the lake. The fishery is managed under statewide regulations with the exception of largemouth bass, which are managed under a slot limit. Only largemouth bass 14 inches long and less or 18 inches and longer may be retained. Daily bag limit for all black bass is 5 in any combination of largemouth, smallmouth, or spotted.

Contact: City of Runaway Bay, (940) 575-4745; Wise County Park, (940) 644-1910; Northside Marina, (940) 644-5475; Texas Parks and Wildlife District Office, (903) 786-2389

15 Lake Texoma

Description of area: Texoma is one of the largest lakes in Texas, covering approximately 75,000 surface acres. About two-thirds of the lake actually lies in the neighboring state of Oklahoma. The main tributaries are the Red and Washita Rivers. The lake lies just northwest of Denison, Texas, off US 75. Maximum depth is 100 feet near the dam on the southeastern section of the lake. Water clarity is normally moderately clear and annual fluctuation is 4 to 8 feet. There is approximately 580 miles of shoreline that consists of cut banks, rocky and sandy beaches, and tall bluffs, boulder fields, standing flooded timber, and some extensive areas of aquatic vegetation in shallow coves and multiple islands in the midlake area. The US Army Corps of Engineers is the controlling water body authority.

Major species: Striped bass, white bass, largemouth bass, smallmouth bass, spotted bass, crappie, channel and blue catfish

Rating of fishery: Striped bass, smallmouth bass, and blue catfish are excellent. Largemouth bass, spotted bass, channel catfish, white bass, and crappie are good.

The fishing: Texoma is unique among freshwater lakes in Texas because it is the only water body with a naturally reproducing striper fishery. The Red and Washita Rivers feeding the reservoir provide ideal spawning habitat for these adaptable saltwater fish, which have the ability to survive in certain freshwater habitats year-round. In Texoma they propagate and maintain a phenomenal year-round fishery. Only 8 other lakes worldwide have documented striper spawning on a regular basis. The lake is loaded with striped bass and limits are liberal for these very popular gamefish.

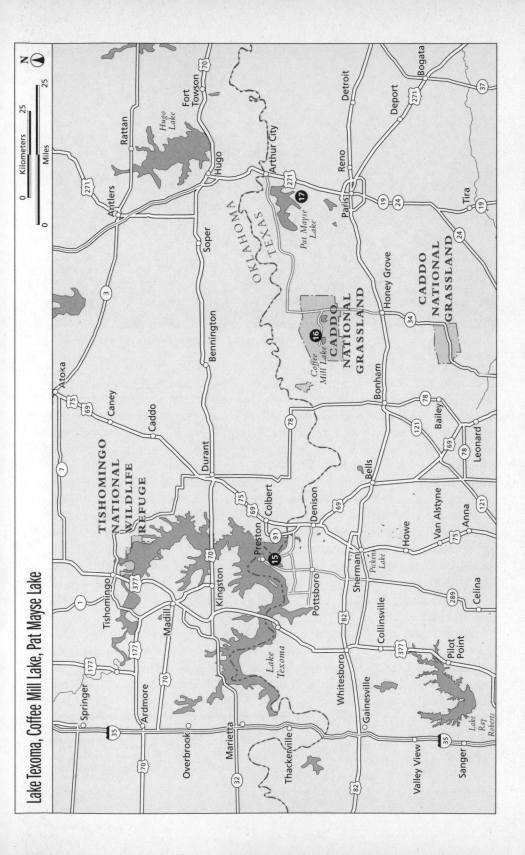

Lake Texoma, Coffee Mill Lake, Pat Mayse Lake

Trolling early in the morning is a proven method to catch striped bass on Lake Texoma.

In the spring they migrate up the rivers to spawn and then follow the river channels back to the main lake and feed on shad on the flats, main lake points, and around the islands located at midlake. Early mornings they can be caught on large top-water lures cast to shoreline structure. During the day, heavy jigs, slabs, spoons, and live shad fished deep account for most catches. Texoma also has an excellent population of smallmouth bass. The best locations to catch them are the rocky bluffs on the Texas side of the impoundment. The Eisenhower Park bluffs, the rip-rap along the dam, and the clearer waters of the Washita River are prime locations. Largemouths are available all over this sprawling reservoir but are most prevalent in coves with aquatic vegetation. White bass also run up the tributaries in the spring and return to main lake points and on the north side of the midlake islands during the summer months. The lake is also well known as a trophy-blue-cat fishery and had the distinction of holding the world record blue catfish caught on rod and reel for a period of time. In 2004 an angler caught a 121.5-pound blue catfish while bank fishing using cut shad for bait.

Note: Based upon recent test results, the blue-green algae warning at Lake Texoma changed to a lake-wide advisory. Primary body contact with the water is discouraged. The lake is open to boating and fishing. Boaters are advised to use caution and avoid direct contact with the water. Fish should be cleaned well and entrails should be discarded, but fish are fine to consume. Check the USACE Tulsa District website www.swt.usace.army.mil for updates.

Directions: From Denison drive north on SH 91 to the Texoma Dam. Turn left on FM 1310 and drive west approximately 2 miles to Park Road 20. Follow to Eisenhower Park. From Pottsboro take FM 120 north about 7 miles to Highport Road, turn left, and follow it 2 miles to Highport Marina.

Map: DeLorme: *Texas Atlas and Gazetteer:* Page 38 B5

Additional information: Numerous private and public parks, marinas, and angler-related services are located along the southern shoreline of Texoma. Call the Pottsboro Chamber of Commerce for detailed information. A special Lake Texoma license is required to fish both Oklahoma and Texas sides of the lake. The fishery is managed under multiple exceptions for bag and length limits. Consult the *Outdoor Annual* or the website listed in the appendix for a list of the laws applicable to this lake.

Contact: Eisenhower State Park, (903) 465-1956; Highport Marina, (903) 786-7000; Pottsboro Chamber of Commerce, (903) 786-6371; Texas Parks and Wildlife District Office, (903) 786-2389

16 Coffee Mill Lake (see map on page 49)

Description of area: Coffee Mill is a small reservoir at 650 surface acres, located in the Caddo National Grassland Wildlife Management Area about 15 miles northeast of the city of Bonham. The controlling authority is the US Forest Service. The lake fluctuates very little on an annual basis and the water clarity is moderately stained. Maximum depth is 30 feet.

Major species: Largemouth bass, channel catfish, crappie, sunfish

Rating of fishery: Crappie, catfish, and sunfish are excellent. Largemouth bass is good.

The fishing: Coffee Mill is locally famous as an outstanding producer of large crappie and a plentiful supply of eating-size channel catfish. Fishery surveys conducted by Texas Parks and Wildlife biologists rate Coffee Mill as having the highest population of crappie in the 8-county area of the district. The easiest time to catch them is in the spring when they move into shallow shoreline areas to spawn. In the winter look for large schools of crappie to congregate on the submerged brush piles near the dam and on other deep-water structure. The shoreline of Coffee Mill is vegetated with water willow, cattails, and pondweed. Spinner baits and top-water lures worked along the edges will pull the largemouth bass out from the cover in the spring. In the summer jigs, crankbaits, and Texas-rigged plastic worms fished around the deeper brush piles, the standing timber in the upper end of the lake, and the ends of points are most effective. Drift-fishing cut bait, shrimp, or blood baits will entice the catfish in this productive reservoir.

Directions: From Bonham drive north on SH 78 approximately 2 miles and turn right on FM 898. Follow it about 5 miles to FM 1396, turn right, and continue approximately 6 miles to FM 2029. Turn north and follow the road approximately 2 miles to FM 409. Turn right and look for the lake entrance sign. Total distance from Bonham is approximately 15 miles.

Map: DeLorme: *Texas Atlas and Gazetteer:* Page 39 D8

Additional information: The park at Coffee Mill is controlled by the US Forest Service. Camping, a 1-lane boat ramp, picnic areas, and restrooms are available. A permit is required. Call the Forest Service for details. The fishery is managed under statewide regulations with one exception: Trotlines, throw lines, and jug lines are not allowed. Local information on angler-related services is available from the Bonham Chamber of Commerce.

Contact: US Forest Service, (940) 627-5475; Bonham Chamber of Commerce, (903) 583-4811; Texas Parks and Wildlife District Office, (903) 786-2389

17 Pat Mayse Lake (see map on page 49)

Description of area: This 6,000-acre reservoir is located on Sanders Creek, a tributary of the Red River 12 miles north of the city of Paris just off US 271. The water level fluctuates 2 to 4 feet annually and remains moderately stained. Maximum depth is 55 feet. The controlling water authority is the US Army Corps of Engineers.

Major species: White bass, hybrid striped bass, largemouth bass, spotted bass, crappie, channel catfish

Rating of fishery: White bass and hybrid striped bass are excellent. Largemouth bass, crappie, and catfish are good. Spotted bass is fair.

The fishing: The upper third of the lake west of Lamar Point is heavily timbered, and the creeks and coves in this area provide excellent habitat for largemouth bass and crappie. Spring is when most anglers target them in this area as they move to shallow edges to spawn. Spinner baits, plastic lizards, and soft-plastic jerk baits work well for triggering strikes. Minnows and small jigs are the preferred choices

Chain pickerel are easily caught on a fly in Pat Mayse Lake.

for catching crappie around the flooded timber and shoreline brush. Catfish are easiest to catch during the early summer when they spawn along the riprap facing the dam. Use a cork and drift cut bait, shrimp, or blood bait along the dam face. Hybrid stripers and white bass can be found near the main lake points and along the deeper water in the dam area. Small top-water lures, slabs in white or chartreuse, or lipless crankbaits will get their attention. Trolling small silver spoons across the ends of points and the creek channels is also a productive method for catching these hard-fighting and tasty fish. Anglers who want to catch spotted bass have the best luck fishing small plastic grubs and worms along the dam face. Pat Mayse Lake also contains a population of native chain pickerel. Fly fishermen can catch them along the weedy shorelines in the backs of coves on brightly colored streamers. They do not grow large but are great fun to catch on light tackle. The state record for the species was caught from this lake and weighed 4.75 pounds.

Directions: Take US 271 north from Paris and travel 12 miles to FM 906. Turn left and follow approximately 1 mile to Saunders Cove Road. Turn left and the lake entrance is on the right.

Map: DeLorme: Texas Atlas and Gazetteer: Page 39 C11

Additional information: The US Army Corps of Engineers maintains and operates 4 parks around Pat Mayse with boat ramps, campgrounds, bathrooms with showers, and picnic facilities. Call them for details and a free lake map. The fishery is managed under statewide regulations with no exceptions. Other angler-related services are available in the nearby town of Powderly on US 271 at the FM 906 turnoff.

Contact: US Army Corps of Engineers, (903) 732-3020; Texas Parks and Wildlife District Office, (903) 593-5077

18 Gibbons Creek Reservoir

Description of area: Gibbons Creek is a power-plant-cooling lake located in Grimes County about 20 miles east of the cities of Bryan and College Station in central Texas. It sits on a tributary of the Navasota River near the town of Carlos just off SH 30. Maximum surface area is 2,770 acres and at its deepest point measures 34 feet. Annual water fluctuation is 1 to 2 feet and the lake remains slightly to moderately stained year-round. The Texas Municipal Power Agency is the controlling entity.

Major species: Largemouth bass; channel, blue, and flathead catfish; crappie

Rating of fishery: Largemouth bass and all 3 species of catfish are excellent. Crappie is good.

The fishing: Largemouth bass are what draw most anglers to this power-plant-cooling reservoir. The lake has been heavily stocked for a number of years, and catches of bass over 10 pounds are quite common. The lake record is over 16 pounds, and late winter to early spring is when most catches of large bass are made at Gibbons. Bass move to the warmwater discharge areas to spawn and become more available to anglers fishing the shoreline. Crankbaits, top waters, and spinner baits are top

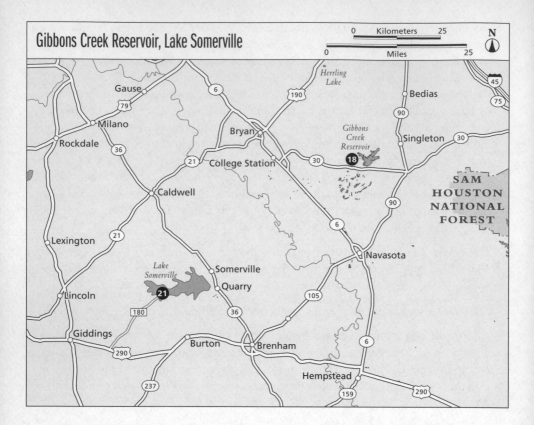

Gibbons Creek Reservoir, Lake Somerville

producers of trophy bass. The shoreline has adequate vegetation for bass habitat and there are some coves and creeks with thick standing timber and dense grass beds. During the hot months Carolina-rigged plastic creature baits worked around deep-water creek channels and points are one of the most productive techniques for getting into hungry fish. Crappie populations are not high in Gibbons, but the fish that are present tend to be larger as a result. Catfish populations and the overall size of them are excellent in this small impoundment. Drift fishing natural or prepared baits is a popular method for sacking them up. Fishing with live bait near the warm-water discharge area is a good way to tie into large flatheads.

Directions: From College Station travel east on SH 30 for 20 miles to Carlos. Turn left on FM 244 and follow to boat ramp.

Map: DeLorme: Texas Atlas and Gazetteer: Page 71 C8

Additional information: No trotlines, throw lines, or jug lines are allowed on Gibbons Creek. Statewide regulations apply in this lake with one exception: Largemouth bass are managed under a slot limit. Bass 14 inches and less or 24 inches or greater may be retained. Only 1 bass 24 inches or larger may be kept each day. The Bryan–College Station Convention and Visitors Bureau can provide local information on lodging and other necessary angler services.

Contact: Texas Municipal Power Agency, (903) 873-2424; Texas Parks and Wildlife District Office, (979) 822-5067; Bryan–College Station Convention and Visitors Bureau, (979) 260-9898 or (800) 777-8292

19 Lake Whitney

Description of area: Lake Whitney is an impoundment formed by damming the Nolan and Brazos Rivers approximately 30 miles north and west of the city of Waco, just off SH 22. The lake is extensive in length, following the old river channel among high limestone bluffs interspersed with agricultural lands, and extends over 23,000 acres. Maximum depth is 108 feet and water clarity is somewhat stained year-round. Typical water level fluctuations are 4 to 8 feet, but heavy rains in 2007 filled the lake to capacity and flooded some parks around the shoreline. The US Army Corps of Engineers is the water body authority and maintains several parks around the reservoir.

Major species: Striped bass, white bass, largemouth bass, smallmouth bass, crappie, blue and channel catfish

Rating of fishery: Striped bass, white bass, catfish, and smallmouth bass are excellent. Largemouth bass and crappie are good.

The fishing: Lake Whitney was one of the best striper lakes in Texas until a series of golden alga outbreaks in 2000 and 2001 reduced the population of these popular gamefish. The lake was restocked and in 2007 anglers reported catching legal-size

Rocky points and bluff ledges on Lake Whitney provide excellent habitat for striped, smallmouth, and largemouth bass.

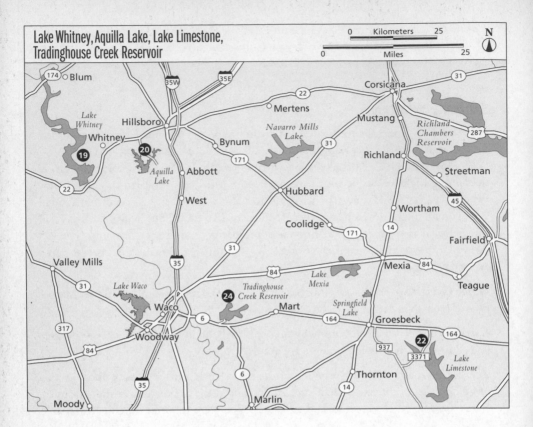

Lake Whitney, Aquilla Lake, Lake Limestone,
Tradinghouse Creek Reservoir

striped bass (18 inches) again. The trend looks positive for this once mighty striper fishery to recover and produce large fish again. Trolling jigs and drifting live shad along the river channels and adjacent flats are 2 productive methods for catching stripers on Whitney. Other species present in Whitney were not as severely impacted by the alga outbreak as were the stripers. Fishing for white bass, catfish, and smallmouth bass remains excellent and the largemouth fishing is still good. The best largemouth fishing occurs during the spring spawning season when the fish are in shallow water.

A state record smallmouth bass that weighed 7.77 pounds was caught by an angler fishing Whitney in 1988. That record lasted for 10 years until a larger bass was caught from Lake Meredith in the Texas Panhandle. White bass make an annual run from the lake up the Nolan and Brazos Rivers in late winter and provide excellent fishing opportunities for both boat and bank anglers. During the summer they gather in large schools on main lake points and feed on the surface, providing exciting top-water fishing using small crankbaits and slabs. Smallmouth bass are found along the rocky shorelines and points from the midlake area to the dam and respond to weighted grubs, jigs, and crayfish-pattern crankbaits. Wintertime trophy fishing for large blue catfish is also one of Whitney's strong points. Cut shad fished along the river channels, rock piles, and timber jams can produce fish up to 60 pounds.

Note: Periodic golden alga blooms occur on this lake. Contact the TPWD District Office for current conditions before visiting.

Directions: From Hillsboro on I-35, exit to SH 22 and follow west to the town of Whitney. The lake lies about 3 miles just south and west of Whitney.

Map: DeLorme: Texas Atlas and Gazetteer: Page 58 C1

Additional information: Whitney is a very scenic and popular recreational area and has many angler-related services available around the lake. The Army Corps of Engineers maintains a dozen parks around the lake and there are private facilities as well. Contact the Corps and Lake Whitney Chamber of Commerce for details. Fishing is managed under statewide regulations with no exceptions.

Contact: US Army Corps of Engineers, (254) 694-3189; Lake Whitney Chamber of Commerce, (254) 694-2540; Texas Parks and Wildlife District Office, (254) 666-5190

20 Aquilla Lake (see map on page 56)

Description of area: Located on Aquilla Creek 35 miles north of Waco, Aquilla Lake is a 3,000-surface-acre reservoir under the control of the US Army Corps of Engineers. Maximum depth is 60 feet and annual water fluctuation ranges between 2 and 4 feet. The water clarity is usually somewhat stained. Fish habitat consists of some aquatic vegetation in the coves and abundant amounts of standing timber and flooded brush in the main tributaries. There are numerous brush piles and stump fields, old tree lines, and fence rows.

Major species: Largemouth bass, white bass, crappie, catfish

Rating of fishery: Largemouth bass, crappie, and catfish are good. White bass is fair.

The fishing: The combination of stained water and large amounts of brushy cover in shallow water areas can combine for excellent opportunities to catch largemouth bass in Aquilla. Working the brush lines with spinner baits, top waters, jerk baits, jigs, and soft-plastic creature baits is a productive tactic. Because of the stained water in the creek arms, bass stay shallow in Aquilla, but spring, when they are spawning, is the best time to fish for them around shoreline cover and in the backs of coves. Crappie anglers target the timbered flats, shoreline brush, dam riprap, and old road bridges with minnows and jigs. Hot spot areas include the FM 1947 Bridge and the Aquilla Creek road bed. White bass anglers do well fishing the riprap along the dam drifting live or cut shad. The deep humps near the dam are another hot spot during the summer and fall. Bouncing a jig or spoon on the old road bed across Aquilla Creek is also a productive tactic. Fishing near the aerator and around Snake Island with chrome-colored lipless crankbaits is also popular. Catfish are abundant and can be caught on cut shad or chicken liver along the riprap at the dam and the old road bed.

Directions: From Hillsboro, travel south on SH 22 approximately 6 miles to Peoria and turn left on FM 1947. Cross the dam and the Dairy Hill Ramp is on the right. No fee required to launch.

Map: DeLorme: Texas Atlas and Gazetteer: Page 58 C1

Secondary and main lake points are hot spots for largemouth bass on Aquilla Lake.

Additional information: Two free ramps are available on Aquilla and there is a no-fee fishing pier located at the spillway. All are operated by the Army Corps of Engineers. There are no camping facilities on the lake. The closest store with angler-related services is located in Peoria on SH 22 and FM 1947. The fishery is managed under statewide regulations with an exception for largemouth bass. The daily bag limit is 5 fish per day and they must be a minimum of 18 inches in length to retain.

Contact: US Army Corps of Engineers, (254) 694-3189; Texas Parks and Wildlife District Office, (254) 666-5190; Hillsboro Chamber of Commerce, (254) 582-2481

21 Lake Somerville (see map on page 54)

Description of area: Somerville is a fairly shallow impoundment of 11,500 surface acres located on Yegua Creek, approximately 30 miles southwest of the cities of Bryan/College Station. Maximum depth is 38 feet and water levels fluctuate 1 to 6 feet annually. Water clarity is usually somewhat stained. The lake is controlled by the US Army Corps of Engineers. Fish habitat consists of shoreline vegetation, stump fields, points, drop-offs, creek channels, riprap, old road beds, and rock quarries.

Major species: Hybrid striped bass, white bass, largemouth bass, catfish, crappie

Rating of fishery: White and hybrid striped bass and catfish are excellent. Largemouth bass and crappie are good.

The fishing: White bass make an annual spawning run up Yegua Creek when water flows coincide with their annual late-winter migration up tributaries. Small crankbaits, spinners, and jigs are all productive lures. Hybrids can be caught in the creek mouths and points on the main creek arms during this period too. Slabs, spoons, and swim baits fished close to the bottom are steady producers. Whites and hybrids will move back to main lake structure in March. Good places to locate them are on main lake points such as Rocky Creek, humps, main lake creek channels, around Snake Island, and the dam area. Drifting live shad close to the bottom is a very productive tactic. They can also be caught bouncing a slab in chrome, white, or chartreuse on the bottom. Trolling shad-imitating crankbaits will also put fish in the boat in those same areas.

Largemouth bass fishing is best in the spring in the creek arms and coves around rocks, tree jams, shoreline vegetation, riprap along the dam, and stump fields in the Oaks area. Spinner baits, soft-plastic creature baits worked along shoreline cover, and jigs fished around the stumps are good lures to fool them. After spawning they will relocate to road beds, humps, creek channels, main lake points, and other deep-water structure. Crankbaits, jigs, and Carolina-rigged plastic worms are the go-to lures. Crappie anglers target their favorite fish with minnows and jigs in the Little Crappie Point and Big Island Point areas in spring. In early summer look for them to be around Deer Island, the Pecan Lake area, and the stumps in the Oaks area. Catfish are abundant and easy to catch on dough baits or cut shad in the creek channels in Brushy and Burns Creek, and around the Birch Creek humps.

Directions: From Giddings travel east approximately 7 miles on US 290 to FM 180. Turn north and follow for 13 miles to Lake Somerville State Park ramp. Fee required.

Map: DeLorme: Texas Atlas and Gazetteer: Page 47 K10

Additional information: Access and camping areas are abundant on Lake Somerville. The Corps of Engineers operates 3 parks with camping and other angler-related services. Call for details. Texas Parks and Wildlife maintains a 2-unit state park, and the city of Somerville and private operators also provide camping and other services around the lake. The fishery is managed under statewide regulations with no exceptions.

Contact: Lake Somerville State Park Birch Creek Unit, (979) 535-7763; US Army Corps of Engineers, (979) 596-1622; Texas Parks and Wildlife District Office, (979) 822-5067

22 Lake Limestone (see map on page 56)

Description of area: Spreading across 3 counties and covering 12,500 surface acres, Limestone is not a very deep lake but it is a productive one. It is fed by the Navasota River and lies approximately 15 miles southeast of the city of Groesbeck. The lake is under the control of the Brazos River Authority. Water levels fluctuate 1 to 3 feet annually and the clarity is somewhat stained. Fish habitat is diverse and plentiful. Aquatic vegetation is abundant along shoreline areas and in the many small inlets, points, and coves. Flooded timber and numerous boathouses, docks, and fishing piers also provide excellent habitat.

Note: As of press time, all boat ramps were closed due to low water levels. However, small boats can be launched from the shoreline. Check current conditions before visiting.

Major species: Largemouth bass, crappie, catfish, white bass

Rating of fishery: Fishing for largemouth bass, crappie, catfish, and white bass is very good.

The fishing: Lake Limestone is one of those reservoirs that receive little publicity because it is off the beaten path, which is just fine with the anglers who do come to fish this productive body of water. The lake has an excellent population of gamefish, with largemouth bass and crappie being the most popular species. As with most Texas lakes, spring is the best time to target white bass, largemouth bass, and crappie. This time frame coincides with those species' spawning season. White bass congregate and move up into the Navasota River in March and April.

They are easily caught on small spinners, jigs, and spoons in the holes and pools as they prepare to spawn. During the summer they school in large numbers and feed on shad along main lake points and the deep-water dam area. Trolling small crankbaits, jigs, and tail spinners will catch them. Vertically jigging slabs or spoons is the best tactic when they are suspended along creek channels or deep-water drop-offs. Largemouth bass anglers concentrate on the shallow coves and creek channels in the spring, when bass move shallow to spawn. Spinner baits, top waters, jigs, and plastic creature baits fished along shoreline vegetation will take fish. In the summer bass move to creek channels, main lake points, and man-made structures along the shoreline with deep-water escape routes nearby. Deep-diving crankbaits, jigs, and Carolina-rigged plastic worms are productive lures to entice them.

Crappie fishermen do very well in early spring fishing flooded vegetation and woody cover in the backs of coves. Minnows and jigs are the preferred bait choices. After spawning, crappie will relocate to creek channels and main lake points with woody cover. Fishing for them in 10 to 20 feet of water using small jigs and minnows is the most productive method. Catfish are easiest to catch in late spring to early summer, when they are spawning and aggressive. Bottom or drift rigs using cut bait or prepared baits will attract them. The edges of creek channels and adjacent flats are good places to find the whisker fish.

Directions: From Groesbeck travel southeast on FM 937 approximately 15 miles to FM 3371. Turn left and continue to Limestone County Park #3.

Map: DeLorme: Texas Atlas and Gazetteer: Page 58 G6

Additional information: The Brazos River Authority and Limestone County maintain 4 public parks on Limestone. They feature all-weather boat ramps with no access fee. None offer camping, electricity, or water. Two private facilities, Running Branch Marina and Limestone Marina, offer full-service camping facilities, cabins, and other angler-related services. The fishery is managed under statewide regulations with no exceptions.

Contact: Brazos River Authority, (903) 529-2141; Running Branch Camp and Marina, (254) 729-5474; Limestone Marina, (800) 636-4119; Texas Parks and Wildlife District Office, (254) 666-5190

23 Lake Benbrook (see map on page 62)

Description of area: Located just 10 miles south of the city of Fort Worth, Benbrook is an urban lake with excellent fishing. Impounded on the Clear Fork of the Trinity River, the lake surface area is approximately 3,700 acres at normal pool. Maximum depth is 70 feet and water levels fluctuate 3 to 4 feet annually under normal rainfall conditions. Water clarity is usually somewhat stained. Aquatic vegetation is limited. Fish-attracting structure consists of flooded timber, rocky ridges, points, and underwater humps and creek channels. The Army Corps of Engineers is the controlling authority.

Note: Due to low water levels, at press time all boat ramps were closed. Small boats can still launch from the shoreline. Check current conditions before visiting.

Major species: Largemouth bass, white bass, hybrid striped bass, crappie, blue and channel catfish

Rating of fishery: Largemouth bass is fair. White bass, crappie, and catfish are good. Hybrid striped bass is excellent.

The fishing: Lake Benbrook gets a lot of pressure on its largemouth bass population due to its close proximity to a major Texas city, but it does produce some nice fish. The lake record for bass is over 13 pounds. Over 300,000 bass fingerlings were stocked in 2006 and 2007. The best time to target bass is spring when the fish move to shallow coves and the mouths of creeks to spawn. Top-water lures, spinner baits, and plastic worms fished near spawning cover are good tactics to find aggressive fish. During the summer jigs, deep-diving crankbaits, and Carolina-rigged creature baits fished on main lake points, humps and ridges, and timbered creek channels are most productive.

White bass move up the tributaries in late winter to spawn and are easily duped by small shad-imitating crankbaits, spinners, spoons, and jigs. During the summer they can be found in large schools around deep-water humps and creek channels. Vertically jigging a spoon or slab on suspended fish will catch them. Hybrid striped bass are most easily caught during late spring through the summer, fishing main lake points, humps, and ridges in deep water on the dam end of the lake. Trolling crankbaits, spinner jigs, and drifting live shad are all productive methods for catching them. Hybrids have been stocked annually since 2002 and provide excellent angling opportunities on Benbrook. Crappie fishing is best in the early spring during their spawn, when they move to brushy shorelines. Look for them in the mouths of tributaries and the backs of coves. A minnow or small jig under a bobber is a deadly tactic for attracting them. In the summer find them holding along timbered creek channels and suspended on rock piles and ridges in 10 to 20 feet of water. Catfish are usually easy to locate by drift-fishing cut bait along the creek channels and nearby flats or using a bottom rig with prepared cheese bait.

Directions: From Fort Worth take US 377 southwest for approximately 10 miles. Turn left on Stevens Road and follow to the Veterans of Foreign Wars building. Turn left and follow for about 0.5 mile to Benbrook Marina.

Map: DeLorme: Texas Atlas and Gazetteer: Page 45 H12

Additional information: Six major public park areas are available around Benbrook. Five are operated by the Army Corps of Engineers and one, Benbrook Marina, is private. All offer boat ramps and related facilities. Benbrook and Rocky Creek Marinas offer enclosed fishing barges for angler use for a fee. Fees are required at all parks except Longhorn, where launching is free. Contact the Army Corps of Engineers Office or Benbrook Marina for details. In addition, many other angler-related services are available around the lake. Call the Fort Worth Convention and Visitors Bureau for more information about the area. The fishery on Benbrook is subject to statewide regulations with no exceptions.

Contact: US Army Corps of Engineers, (817) 292-2400; Benbrook Marina, (817) 249-1173; Fort Worth Convention and Visitors Bureau, (817) 336-8791 or (800) 433-5747; Texas Parks and Wildlife District Office, (817) 732-0761

24 Tradinghouse Creek Reservoir (see map on page 56)

Description of area: Tradinghouse Creek Reservoir is a 2,000-acre power-plant-cooling lake that lies just east of the city of Waco on FM 2957. Maximum depth is 42 feet and the lake water levels fluctuate between 1 and 3 feet in a year of average rainfall. Water clarity is normally stained as the watershed and lake basin are composed of heavy clay soils. Texas Utilities is the controlling water authority. The shorelines are heavily vegetated with cattails, bulrushes, and water lotus and there is hydrilla present also. The lake has no facilities other than 2 public boat ramps located on the south shore.

Note: As of press time, the dry conditions across Texas resulted in all public ramps being closed on Tradinghouse. Small boats can be launched from shore. Check current conditions before visiting.

Major species: Largemouth bass, channel catfish, red drum, crappie

Rating of fishery: Red drum, largemouth bass, and catfish populations are good; crappie is fair.

The fishing: Since 1999, Tradinghouse has been stocked with 100,000 to 300,000 red drum fingerlings annually. Red drum, also known as redfish, are a saltwater species that can thrive in certain freshwater power-plant lakes that have water quality that meets their needs. This fishery is put-and-take as red drum cannot reproduce in freshwater. They grow rapidly and most reach legal size of 20 inches in about 3 years. Anglers typically catch them trolling large deep-diving crankbaits or drift fishing live shad or small sunfish. They will also bite cut bait fished on the bottom.

Catches of these hard-fighting and tasty gamefish up to 20 pounds are not uncommon. They require stout tackle to battle and land successfully. Medium-to-heavy rods of 6 to 7 feet and at least a 20-pound test line are recommended. Most fishing for largemouth bass occurs along the amply vegetated shoreline. The best fishing is during the spawning season. Due to the artificial warmth generated by the power plant, this event starts in early winter. Spinner baits, plastic worms, and top-water lures worked along the edges and over the top of vegetation are how most bass are caught. Crankbaits and jigs fished along the riprap of the dam are also good tactics for catching them. Catfish can be caught drifting cut bait or using prepared stink baits on the bottom.

Directions: From Waco travel east on SH 6 approximately 15 miles to the town of Hallsburg to FM 2957. Turn left and continue on FM 2957 to the county park.

Map: DeLorme: Texas Atlas and Gazetteer: Page 58 F3

Additional information: The boat ramps are maintained by McLennan County and are open year-round. Launching is free. The fishery is managed under statewide

Heavily vegetated shorelines are primary areas to find hungry largemouth bass on Tradinghouse Creek Reservoir.

regulations with one exception: Red drum must be 20 inches in length to be retained and the bag limit is 3 per day per person. There is no maximum size limit. The lake also contains triploid grass carp for vegetation control. If caught, they must be released immediately.

Contact: Texas Utilities, (214) 812-8699; Texas Parks and Wildlife District Office, (254) 666-5190; Waco Chamber of Commerce, (254) 752-6551

25 Lake Belton

Description of area: Belton is a 12,385-acre impoundment on the Leon River 5 miles northwest of the city of Belton. Maximum depth is 124 feet and water levels fluctuate 3 to 5 feet annually. The clarity of the water is moderate. Shorelines consist of rocky bluffs, boulder-strewn points, and broad sandy beaches. There is very little aquatic vegetation and almost no standing timber present.

Major species: Hybrid striped bass, white bass, largemouth bass, smallmouth bass, channel and flathead catfish

Rating of fishery: Hybrid striper fishing is excellent. Largemouth bass and white bass are good. Smallmouth bass and catfish are fair.

The fishing: Lake Belton is known for its excellent hybrid striper fishing. For the past several decades, the lake has been heavily stocked annually with this adaptable species. The lake record is 13.5 pounds. Drifting live shad along the river channel and over the ends of points is a favorite tactic. Trolling shad-imitating crankbaits, spoons, and jigs are also productive techniques. Hybrids also feed on the surface early and late in the day and are easily caught with top-water lures or slabs worked quickly. Peak season for catching largemouth bass is late winter to early spring when the fish

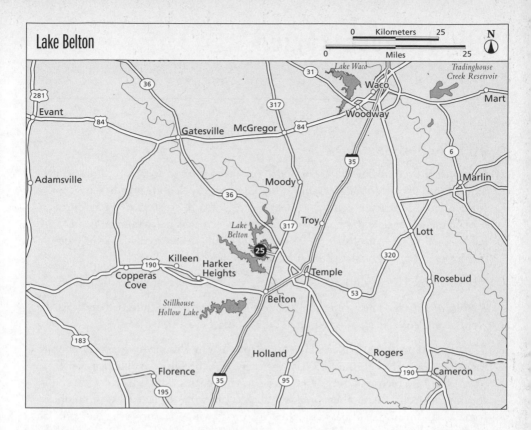

Lake Belton

move to shallow areas to spawn. Productive lures include spinner baits, Texas-rigged plastic worms, buzz baits, and top-water lures worked along shoreline areas and the backs of coves. The highest concentration of smallmouth bass can be found from the midlake area to the dam. Rocky points, boulder piles, and ledges provide good habitat. Deep-diving crayfish-pattern crankbaits, tube jigs, grubs, and drop-shot rigs are good choices to attract them. White bass are easiest to find and catch during their annual late-winter spawning run up the Leon River. Many of them also spawn on sandy points in the upper main lake. They will strike small spoons, spinners, jigs, and crankbaits. Catfishing is best in late spring to early summer on natural and prepared baits in shallow coves and on flats adjacent to the river channel.

Directions: From Belton drive north on SH 317 to FM 2483, turn west, and follow roadside signs to the lake.

Map: *DeLorme: Texas Atlas and Gazetteer:* Page 57 I12

Additional information: The Corps of Engineers is the controlling water authority and has developed and maintains 11 camping parks with boat ramps around Lake Belton. Three marinas offer angling supplies and fuel. The fishery is managed under statewide regulations with no exceptions.

Contact: US Army Corps of Engineers, (254) 939-2461; Texas Parks and Wildlife District Office, (254) 666-5190; Belton Area Chamber of Commerce, (254) 939-3551

Piney Woods Region

26 Lake Bob Sandlin

Description of area: This Piney Woods region reservoir is located 5 miles southwest of the city of Mount Pleasant on Big Cypress Creek and spreads across 9,000 surface acres. Maximum depth is 65 feet, water levels fluctuate 2 to 3 feet during a normal rainfall year, and water clarity is moderate with visibility ranging from 2 to 4 feet. Shoreline habitat consists of flooded timber and areas of hydrilla. Titus County Freshwater Supply District is the controlling water body authority.

Major species: Largemouth bass, white bass, spotted bass, crappie, catfish, sunfish

Rating of fishery: The white bass fishery is excellent. Largemouth bass, catfish, crappie, and sunfish are good; spotted bass is fair.

The fishing: Largemouth bass fishing is very popular on this medium-size impoundment as the lake has produced 7 bass that have qualified for the ShareLunker Program. The lake record is over 14 pounds for this species. The lack of vegetation is the limiting factor on numbers of bass available, but what the lake lacks in numbers, it makes up for in size of bass available. Spring spawning season is the best time of year to hook up with a double-digit female on Sandlin. Soft-plastic creature lures worked around the stickup timber and the vegetation in the backs of coves and jigs

Large coves with brushy shorelines provide excellent cover on Lake Bob Sandlin.

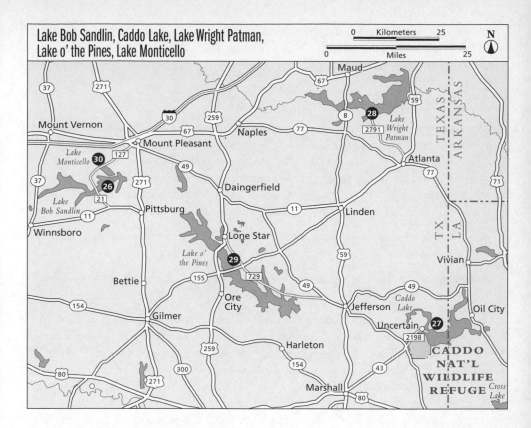

along the timbered creek channels are productive techniques for hanging a big fish. Peak time to catch the lake's abundant white bass is late winter to early spring when they move up the lake and into tributaries to spawn. Small spoons, crankbaits, and jigs in white or chartreuse are favorite patterns. Spotted bass are present in the lake in fair numbers. Small crankbaits and plastic grubs fished deep along creek channels and riprap areas are good choices to entice them. Crappies are most vulnerable in spring when they relocate to shallow shorelines to spawn. Small jigs and minnows under a bobber will catch them. During the summer look for them around standing timber and brush piles in 20 to 25 feet of water. Fishing for channel catfish is best during the early summer along riprap areas and on flats adjacent to creek channels using prepared or cut bait.

Directions: From Mount Pleasant travel south on US 271 to Pittsburg and SH 11. Turn west on SH 21 and travel to FM 1520. Go north for approximately 4 miles, crossing Barefoot Bay, and turn north to Barefoot Bay Marina.

Map: DeLorme: Texas Atlas and Gazetteer: Page 48 D2

Additional information: There are 3 free public boat ramps, a county park, and a state park located on Bob Sandlin that also have launch ramps for a fee. Overnight camping facilities are available in both parks. The fishery is managed under state-wide regulations with no exceptions.

Contact: Barefoot Bay Marina, (903) 856-3643; Bob Sandlin State Park, (903) 572-5531; Texas Parks and Wildlife District Office, (903) 938-1007; Mount Pleasant Chamber of Commerce, (903) 572-8567

27 Caddo Lake (see map on page 67)

Description of area: Caddo Lake is the only naturally occurring lake in Texas. It spreads over approximately 27,000 surface acres with a maximum depth of 20 feet. About one-half of the lake lies in Louisiana. Water levels fluctuate from 4 to 8 feet seasonally and the clarity ranges from moderate to stained. About 95 percent of the lake's surface on the Texas side contains some form of native or exotic vegetation. The lake is filled with bayous and channels rimmed with bald cypress trees.

Major species: Largemouth bass, crappie, catfish, chain pickerel, white and yellow bass, spotted bass

Rating of fishery: Fishing for largemouth bass, crappie, and white bass is excellent. Chain pickerel and catfish are good. Spotted bass is fair.

The fishing: Most anglers come to Caddo for its excellent largemouth bass fishing. The lake has been heavily stocked with Florida bass since 1981by Texas Parks and Wildlife, and catches of bass weighing more than 8 pounds are common. The best fishing for large bass occurs when they build nests in shallow water in late winter to early spring. Plastic lizards and spinner baits are favorite choices for catching them. After spawning the bass will move to the edges of channels and the root systems of the cypress trees and will feed on the spawn of sunfish. Jigs and small crankbaits in bluegill patterns are highly productive in late spring to early summer. Work them along the edges of vegetative cover and the cypress roots. Crappie can be found along shallow edges and tree roots during their spring spawning season. Later they will move to the creek channels and standing timber. Chain pickerel are another native species sought by some anglers for their ferocious attacks on small top-water lures and flies. They prefer the shallow vegetation area, where they can rush out and ambush their prey. They don't grow large (the lake record is 4.6 pounds), but they put up a memorable battle and will leap from the water repeatedly when hooked. White bass are easiest to locate and catch immediately after late winter rains when they will move up small tributaries and to sandy points and islands to spawn. Small jigs or bait rigs with crayfish tails fished on the bottom in areas with current will be irresistible to them. Catfish prowl the channels and flats looking for an easy meal of natural or prepared baits. Best time to sack them up is early summer.

Note: At press time there was a fish consumption advisory for Caddo Lake due to higher than normal levels of mercury in the lake. For largemouth bass and fresh-water drum, adults should limit consumption to no more than two 8-ounce meals per month, and children should limit consumption to no more than two 4-ounce meals per month.

Directions: From Marshall take SH 43 northeast to FM 2198, turn east, and go approximately 1 mile to Caddo Lake State Park.

Map: DeLorme: *Texas Atlas and Gazetteer:* Page 49 H7

Additional information: Two free public ramps are available on Caddo. The state park has a launch ramp and there are numerous private campgrounds and marinas located on the south and west ends of Caddo. The fishery is managed under state-wide regulations except for largemouth bass, which has a 14- to 18-inch slot limit with a 5-fish daily bag limit. Fishing regulations differ on the Louisiana side. Contact the Louisiana Department of Wildlife and Fisheries for information.

Contact: Texas Parks and Wildlife District Office, (903) 938-1007; Caddo Lake Area Chamber of Commerce, (866) 282-2336; Caddo Lake State Park, (903) 679-3351; Louisiana Department of Wildlife and Fisheries, (318) 676-7594

28 Lake Wright Patman (see map on page 67)

Description of area: Wright Patman is a 20,000-surface-acre reservoir impounded on the Sulphur River 10 miles south of the city of Texarkana in northeast Texas. Maximum depth is 40 feet. Water levels fluctuate 3 to 5 feet during an average rainfall year. The clarity remains moderately clear. Very little submerged vegetation is available but shallow areas do have floating and emerged vegetation present. Shoreline areas are covered with willow and button brush. The controlling water authority is the US Army Corps of Engineers.

Major species: Largemouth bass, hybrid striped bass, white bass, crappie, all 3 species of catfish.

Rating of fishery: Hybrid striped bass, white bass, blue catfish, and crappie are excellent. Largemouth bass and flathead catfish are good.

The fishing: Wright Patman is considered an excellent reservoir to catch hybrid striped bass and white bass. Populations of both species are high. The lake has been heavily stocked with hybrids for several years and the resident white bass population combines to make a highly productive fishery for these open water species. Shad-imitating crankbaits, spoons, slabs, and jigs in white or chartreuse are the most productive lures to catch them. Concentrate on the ends of main lake points, creek channels, and humps to locate the schools. In late winter they move into tributaries and the mouths of major coves. During the warm months they follow the river channel and push schools of shad against main lake points, creating exciting top-water fishing opportunities. Largemouth bass fishing is best in the spring during spawning season as the fish move into shallow areas near cover. Typical bass attractors including spinner baits, lipless crankbaits, and plastic worms and jerk baits will all take fish. During the summer months concentrate on creek channels and the ends of points and deep-water timbered areas with jigs and Carolina-rigged plastic worms. Crappie will be shallow in late spring when reproducing and are easily caught using jigs and minnows under bobbers. During the summer they will hold in timbered areas along creek channels, boat docks, and on brush piles in 20 to 25 feet of water. Catfish can be caught during the warm months on prepared baits and cut bait along riprap areas and flats adjacent to creek channels.

Directions: From Atlanta, take SH 77 northwest and travel to Midway. Turn right on FM 2791 and drive north for about 5 miles to Jackson Creek.

Map: DeLorme: Texas Atlas and Gazetteer: Page 48 B5

Additional information: Numerous public and private facilities surround the lake, all catering to fishermen and campers. These include state and county parks with full-service facilities and ramps. All require a fee except the ramp at Overcup Landing just north of Douglassville off SH 8. The fishery is managed under statewide regulations with no exceptions. The US Army Corps of Engineers maintains and operates 10 parks around the reservoir.

Contact: US Army Corps of Engineers, (903) 838-8781; Texas Parks and Wildlife District Office, (903) 938-1007; Texarkana Chamber of Commerce, (903) 792-7191; Atlanta State Park, (903) 796-6476

29 Lake o' the Pines (see map on page 67)

Description of area: Lake o' the Pines is a 17,000-acre reservoir 25 miles northeast of Longview on Big Cypress Creek. Maximum depth is 50 feet. Water levels fluctuate 4 to 5 feet in an average year and the water remains moderately clear year-round. Multiple creeks in the Big Cypress basin provide excellent habitat for a variety of species. Lake o' the Pines is a very popular fishing destination for anglers wanting to sample an East Texas Piney Woods reservoir. Abundant native and exotic plants cover from 10 to 20 percent of the lake's surface, providing excellent cover for largemouth bass. The lake also has many areas of standing timber along flooded creek channels, which helps maintain the excellent crappie fishery.

Major species: Largemouth bass; crappie; white bass; blue, channel, and flathead catfish; chain pickerel; spotted bass

Rating of fishery: Largemouth bass, crappie, and catfish are excellent. Blue and flathead catfish are good. Spotted bass is fair.

The fishing: Largemouth bass and crappie are the 2 main species that attract the majority of anglers to the Pines. The lake has plenty of vegetation that makes topwater lure fishing for bass a very popular activity. Multiple creeks offer ideal habitat for bass and crappie too. Spring spawning season is the easiest time of the year to target the abundant bass population as they move to the backs of creeks and along shorelines to build nests and lay eggs. During the rest of the year, they will be along vegetated creeks and ditches and in the standing timber lining the flooded tributary channels. Top waters, spinner baits, and soft-plastic worms in dark colors and jigs in black and blue are top producers. Crappie are easy pickings when they spawn along shorelines and creeks lined with button brush and willows. During the summer they relocate to timbered areas along creek channels and on brush piles in deeper water. Jigs in contrasting colors and minnows will tempt them into striking. Riprap areas are favorites for catfish anglers using prepared or cut bait on drift rigs. White bass can usually be located along the main creek channels in the lower end of the

Lake o' the Pines sports an excellent crappie fishery, especially during the winter months.

lake and on major points. Small shad-imitating spoons, slabs, and crankbaits are the most productive lures. Spotted bass anglers concentrate on riprap banks and creek channels. Small grubs, jigs, and plastic worms in dark colors fished on the bottom are good choices to fool them.

Directions: From Lone Star just south of Daingerfield, follow US 259 south to FM 729 and turn left before the bridge crossing Big Cypress Creek. Follow FM 729 for approximately 1 mile to the free ramp at Lone Star Landing.

Map: *DeLorme: Texas Atlas and Gazetteer:* Page 48 G4

Additional information: The US Army Corps of Engineers maintains and operates several parks with full-service camping facilities around the reservoir. There are also 5 free ramps available as well as private campgrounds and marinas that charge a fee for launching. The fishery is managed under statewide regulations with one exception. From December 1 through the last day of February, there is no minimum length limit for crappie. Daily bag limit is 25 fish per person and all crappie caught must be kept toward the bag limit. The rest of the year, minimum length limit is 10 inches and bag limit is 25 per person per day.

Contact: US Army Corps of Engineers, (903) 665-2336; Texas Parks and Wildlife District Office, (903) 938-1007; Lake o' the Pines Area Chamber of Commerce, (877) 347-4567

30 Lake Monticello (see map on page 67)

Description of area: Monticello is a power-plant-cooling reservoir operated by Texas Utilities approximately 10 miles southwest of the city of Mount Pleasant. Surface area of the lake is 2,000 acres. Average water level fluctuation is minimal at 2 to 3 feet annually and the water remains moderately clear. Maximum depth is 40 feet. Aquatic vegetation present is primarily hydrilla and American lotus (lily pads), with some reed beds and cattail areas along the shorelines and the shallow northern end of the lake. Riprap along the dam face also provides good cover for gamefish.

Major species: Largemouth bass, channel catfish, sunfish

Rating of fishery: Largemouth bass and channel catfish are excellent. Sunfish, including bluegill and red-ear, is good.

The fishing: Largemouth bass fishing is the draw on Monticello. In 1980 the state record for largemouth bass that had lasted for 37 years and weighed 13.5 pounds was shattered by a bass caught from Monticello that weighed 14.09 pounds. That catch not only bested the most coveted angling record in Texas, it ushered in a new era of fishing for trophy bass in the Lone Star State. The fish is still the lake record to this day. Monticello is still a quality bass fishery and is most popular in the winter because of the high population of largemouth bass and the artificially heated water that keeps bass active during a traditional period of winter lethargy present in other impoundments. Bass accelerate their spawning season several months earlier in Monticello than in non-heated reservoirs. The result is springtime-like fishing opportunities in shallow water during the winter. Top waters, jigs, spinner baits, and jerk baits fished along shorelines and the edges of vegetation are reliable lure choices for catching bass on nests. Later in the year, drop-shot rigs fished on the creek channels and main lake points will tempt them. Crayfish-colored crankbaits fished along the dam riprap are also a productive technique. Channel catfish can be caught just about anywhere on cheese and other prepared baits. The lake also holds some very large flathead catfish. Live sunfish drifted along the creek channels and the dam face is one of the best means of catching them.

Directions: From Mount Pleasant travel southwest on FM 127. Cross the lake and continue to CR 2710. Turn left and follow approximately 2 miles to Titus County Park. A fee is required to launch at the ramp.

Map: DeLorme: Texas Atlas and Gazetteer: Page 48 D1

Additional information: Titus County maintains and operates the only park and boat ramp at the lake. A camping area is available. The fishery is managed under statewide regulations with one exception for largemouth bass. There is a slot limit on bass. Bass 14 inches and less or 24 inches or longer in length may be kept, with a daily bag limit of 5 fish per person. Only 1 bass 24 inches or longer may be kept daily.

Contact: Titus County Park, (903) 572-2398; Texas Parks and Wildlife District Office, (903) 938-1007; Mount Pleasant Chamber of Commerce, (903) 572-8567

Fishing power plant reservoirs such as Lake Monticello during the winter allows anglers an opportunity to hook up with big fish.

31 Lake Fork (see map on page 38)

Description of area: Situated on Lake Fork Creek between Emory and Quitman, Lake Fork has the reputation of being the best trophy-bass-fishing lake in the United States and maybe the world. Surface area is just over 27,000 acres, maximum depth is 70 feet. Water levels fluctuate between 2 and 4 feet annually and the water clarity remains moderately clear year-round. The lake has a very irregular shoreline and is fed by many small tributaries. Aquatic vegetation is abundant in coves and secondary points. A lot of standing timber exists in the Caney and Lake Fork Creek arms north and northeast of the dam. Boat lanes have been cut and buoyed to help anglers navigate, but care should be taken to avoid trees just under the water line in many areas. The Sabine River Authority is the controlling water body authority.

Major species: Largemouth bass, crappie, channel and blue catfish

Rating of fishery: Largemouth bass and crappie fishing is excellent. Catfish is good.

The fishing: Anglers come from all over the world to sample the bass fishing on Fork. More than half of the 50 largest bass caught in the state have come from Fork. These include the former record, a 17.67-pound fish, and the current record bass that weighed 18.18 pounds. Bass over 10 pounds rarely raise an eyebrow of interest from local anglers since more than 200 bass have been caught from Fork that weighed at least 13 pounds.

Winter to early spring is the best time of the year to set the hook on a double-digit fish, but they do get caught year-round. Fishing the beds in shallow water during the spawn is the best bet for hanging a trophy. Plastic lizards, jigs, and

Main lake points on Lake Fork are hot spots for largemouth bass fishing.

Crappie hot spots on Lake Fork are easily found during the winter season; look for a cluster of boats and join in.

spinner baits are all good lures for tricking a big sow into biting. During the summer bass relocate to weed beds along creek channels, timbered creeks, main lake points, and humps in the main lake. Carolina rigs and deep-diving crankbaits are what it takes to catch them. In the fall they move into the mouths of coves following the seasonal movement of baitfish. Crankbaits and plastic jerk baits are good producers of strikes. Crappie fishing is also a major draw on Fork.

In the spring they move to shallow brushy shorelines, brush piles, and boat docks to spawn. They become easy prey for anglers armed with long rods, jigs, and minnows. Four bridges that cross various parts of the lake also provide prime habitat between spring spawning and their relocation to deep-water areas near the dam during the cold season. During the winter thousands of these tasty gamefish suspend on the humps and flooded timber areas just north of the dam. Small jigs and minnows fished close to the bottom are the preferred method to reach them. Channel catfish are prolific all over the lake and are easily caught on various prepared and natural baits. A developing trophy blue cat fishery also lures many anglers to Fork in the winter. Drifting cut bait along major deep-water creek channels and brush piles is an excellent way to catch blues up to 60 pounds. The lake record is 71 pounds.

Directions: From Emory take US 69 east for 1 mile and turn left on FM 515. Continue for 7 miles to SH 17. Turn right and follow signs to public ramp located on the left.

Map: *DeLorme: Texas Atlas and Gazetteer:* Page 47 G11

Additional information: Fork is subject to special regulations for largemouth bass. A slot limit of 16 to 24 inches is in effect. Bass 16 inches or less in length or 24 inches or longer may be kept. Daily bag limit is 5 bass. Only 1 bass 24 inches or longer may be kept per day. Crappie are also subject to special rules. From December 1 to the last day of February, there is no minimum length limit and all crappie caught must be kept up to 25 per person per day. The remainder of the year, the minimum length for crappie is 10 inches, 25 fish per person per day. The lake is ringed with angler-related businesses, and the Sabine River Authority maintains 4 public boat ramps with no fees and a day-use area.

Contact: Texas Parks and Wildlife District Office, (903) 593-5077; Sabine River Authority, (903) 878-2262; Lake Fork Area Chamber of Commerce, (903) 780-6595

32 Lake Murvaul

Description of area: Situated 15 miles east of the city of Carthage, Murvaul is an old and very productive largemouth bass fishery impounded on a bayou that spreads across 3,400 surface acres. Water clarity is moderately clear and levels fluctuate a modest 2 to 3 feet annually. Maximum depth is 36 feet and the lake supports an aquatic plant population that covers from 10 to 30 percent of its surface, providing ideal habitat for largemouth bass. Panola County Freshwater District is the controlling water authority.

Major species: Largemouth bass, crappie, channel catfish, sunfish

Rating of fishery: Largemouth bass and channel catfish are excellent. Crappie and sunfish are good.

The fishing: Lake Murvaul is a small but highly productive reservoir tucked away in the piney woods of East Texas. Most anglers come to fish for largemouth bass, and the current lake record for the species is over 14 pounds. Typically, bass fishing is best from late winter to midspring in shallow areas when fish are spawning and more vulnerable to anglers fishing shoreline cover. Top-water lures, spinner baits, and soft-plastic creature baits catch the majority of fish. During the summer and winter, bass retreat to creek channels and the ends of main lake points. Jigs and Carolina-rigged plastic worms are good choices to catch them. Boat docks and rip-rap areas also hold fish during the warmwater seasons. Bass over 8 pounds are common on Murvaul. Crappie fishing is very good on jigs and minnows fished along the timbered creek channels and around boat docks and the pilings under the FM 1971 Bridge. This lake teems with channel catfish and they readily bite on natural and prepared baits during the warm months. Flats near creek channels and riprap areas are steady producers of hefty stringers of the whisker fish.

Directions: From Carthage take SH 315 southwest to Clayton. Turn left on FM 1970 and follow to FM 1234. Continue to Decker-Hill Park.

Additional information: Lake Murvaul was the first lake in Texas to be stocked with the Florida-strain largemouth bass, in the 1970s. The lake's fishery is managed

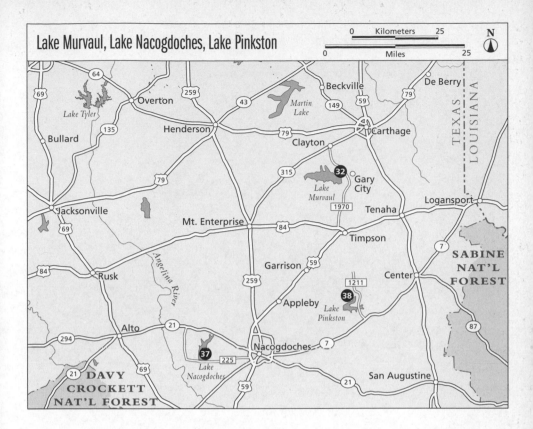

0   Kilometers   25

0   Miles   25

N

under statewide regulations except for largemouth bass, which have a slot limit in effect to protect the larger fish from harvest. Bass 14 inches and less or 21 inches or longer may be retained, with a daily bag limit of 5 fish per angler. Only 1 bass 21 inches or longer may be kept daily. Four launch ramps are available around the lake and 2 parks offer camping facilities. All are maintained and operated by the Panola County Freshwater District and there is no launch fee, but camping fees are required.

Contact: Panola County Freshwater District, (903) 693-6562; Texas Parks and Wildlife District Office, (903) 938-1007; Panola County Chamber of Commerce, (903) 693-6634

33 Lake Toledo Bend (see map on page 78)

Description of area: Toledo Bend is the largest reservoir in Texas at 181,000 surface acres. The lake shares its eastern border with Louisiana. Maximum depth is 110 feet and typical water fluctuation is 1 to 5 feet annually. The upper half of the lake remains slightly turbid while the middle and lower portions are moderately clear. The main tributary is the Sabine River. Toledo Bend is so large it spreads across 3 East Texas counties. The dam at its southern end lies approximately 24 miles north of the city of Jasper. Submerged and emerged vegetation is plentiful

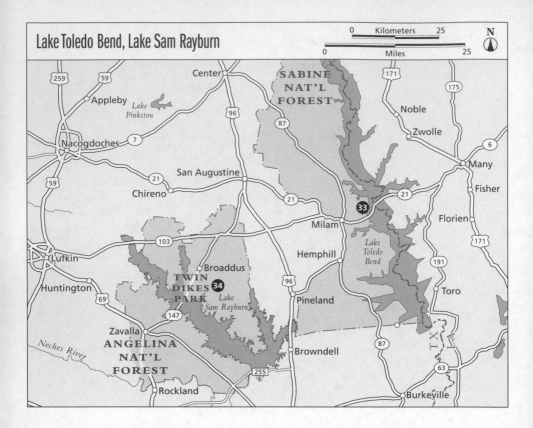

in the middle and southern portions of the lake. The upper end supports mostly shoreline brush species because of the turbid conditions. The shoreline is highly irregular, with many coves and small tributaries, which provide outstanding habitat for largemouth bass and crappie. The Sabine River Authority controls the water in Toledo Bend.

Major species: Largemouth bass, crappie, catfish, white and striped bass

Rating of fishery: Largemouth bass, crappie, and sunfish are excellent. White bass and striped bass are good.

The fishing: This sprawling reservoir is famous for its excellent largemouth bass and crappie fishing. Due to its size, there are nearly limitless areas to fish for them. Starting in late winter, largemouth bass relocate from deep water to shallow areas and build nests to spawn. This is prime time to catch them along shoreline areas and in the backs of creek channels. Top-water lures, jerk baits, spinner baits, and jigs are all good lure choices. Post-spawn fish move to creek channels with timber or vegetation and main lake points. Crankbaits, jigs, and Carolina- or Texas-rigged plastics are the go-to lures for those bass holding in deeper water. Lipless crankbaits and buzz baits worked along the edges of vegetation will also produce exciting action. The lake record for largemouth bass is just over 15 pounds.

Crappie fishing is excellent year-round on small jigs and minnows. Fish the brushy shorelines during their spring spawning season and limits are easy. During the summer timbered creek channels and brush piles in 15 to 25 feet of water will be holding large schools of these tasty gamefish. In the fall crappie move into creek channels and gang up around timber or submerged vegetation, feeding on small shad also on the move. White bass make an annual early spring spawning run up the Sabine River in the northern part of the reservoir. They will gather at the mouth of the river and other flowing tributaries by the thousands and are easily fooled by small spoons, spinners, jigs, and crankbaits. Striped bass are primarily caught in the southern end of Toledo on trolled crankbaits and jigs along main lake points, the river channel, and near the dam. Some top-water action is available in the fall and winter when cooler water temps lure them to the surface.

Directions: From Milam, travel east on SH 21 for 5 miles.

Map: DeLorme: Texas Atlas and Gazetteer: Page 61 H10

Additional information: There are at least 33 angler-related facilities on the Texas side of Toledo Bend. These include parks, marinas, campgrounds, launch ramps, and motels. Contact the Jasper Chamber of Commerce and the Sabine River Authority for details. Anglers who possess a valid Texas fishing license may fish on the Louisiana side of Toledo Bend without penalty. Some size and bag limit regulations differ if launching on the Louisiana side. The fishery on the Texas side of the reservoir is managed under statewide regulations with the following exceptions: Daily bag limit for black bass of all species is 8 fish. Possession limit is 10 fish.

Coves with overhanging vegetation provide excellent cover for largemouth bass on Lake Toledo Bend.

The daily bag and possession limit for crappie is 50 fish. Minimum length limit of 10 inches is in effect March through November. December through January there is no minimum length limit. All crappie caught must be kept during those months. A 5-fish limit per day, of which only 2 fish may be longer than 30 inches, with no minimum length limit, is in effect for striped bass. There is no minimum length limit for white bass, and anglers may keep 25 per person per day.

Contact: Texas Parks and Wildlife District Office, (409) 384-9572; Jasper Chamber of Commerce, (409) 384-2762; Sabine River Authority, (409) 565-2273

34 Lake Sam Rayburn (see map on page 78)

Description of area: Sam Rayburn is a 115,000-acre impoundment located on the Angelina River about 20 miles north of the city of Jasper and 18 miles west of Lake Toledo Bend. Maximum depth is 80 feet. The upper lake is usually stained by inflow from the river, while the lower lake remains moderately clear. The lake levels can fluctuate up to 10 feet annually. The upper end of the lake has little aquatic vegetation in the form of submerged or emerged weed beds, but the lower lake has significant amounts of non-native hydrilla and reasonable amounts of native vegetation that provide excellent largemouth bass habitat. There are stands of submerged timber, and in the spring and winter, inflows many times provide large areas of flooded vegetation along creeks and adjacent shorelines. The controlling water authority is the US Army Corps of Engineers.

Major species: Largemouth bass, crappie, catfish, white and hybrid striped bass

Rating of fishery: Largemouth bass, crappie, and catfish are excellent. White bass and hybrid striped bass are good.

The fishing: Largemouth bass fishing is what compels most anglers to come to Sam Rayburn. At approximately 115,000 acres, Big Sam, as it is affectionately called, offers miles of shoreline habitat attractive to bass. The annual spring season is when most anglers hit the shallows to capitalize on the spawn. Top waters, jigs, soft-plastic lizards, jerk baits, and spinner baits are effective lures. The Florida-strain bass has been heavily stocked into Rayburn for the last 3 decades or so, and the bass population remains high and healthy. During the summer anglers have the best luck fishing weed beds along creek channels, main lake points, and timbered areas with jigs, spoons, and deep-diving crankbaits. Lipless crankbaits fished over the top of submerged grass beds along creeks is also a popular technique.

During the fall top-water and crankbait action picks up in the mouths of creeks with vegetation. Crappie fishing is excellent year-round. Focus on the shallow, brushy areas in the spring. During the summer crappie move to timbered creek channels and brush piles. In the fall they relocate to shallower water around boat docks, brush piles in coves, and creek mouths. When water temperatures plummet in winter, they move to deep-water humps, creek channels, and brush piles. Small jigs in contrasting colors and small minnows are favored baits. Hybrid stripers can be found along the creek channels in the Farmer Flats area, north of the dam, along

Spinner baits are one of the top-producing lures for largemouth bass like this one caught from Lake Sam Rayburn.

the dam face, and on main lake points in the southern portion of the reservoir. Swim baits, jigs, and slabs are all popular lures to catch them. In fall and winter they will surface to chase shad and will hit just about any lure that resembles a small baitfish. White bass make an annual run up the tributaries in late winter and are easily fooled with small jigs, spoons, and crankbaits in white or chartreuse colors. Catfish can be caught all over the lake on stink baits and prepared cheese baits as well as shrimp or cut bait.

Note: As of press time a consumption warning was in effect on Sam Rayburn due to higher than normal levels of mercury. For largemouth bass and freshwater drum, adults should limit consumption to no more than two 8-ounce meals per month, and children should limit consumption to no more than two 4-ounce meals per month.

Directions: From Jasper follow US 96 north for approximately 12 miles. Turn left on FM 255 and continue to Twin Dikes Marina, located on the right about 0.5 mile east of Twin Dikes Park.

Map: DeLorme: Texas Atlas and Gazetteer: Page 61 J7

Additional information: The Army Corps of Engineers operates 13 parks around the reservoir and all of them have launch ramps. Other parks, private marinas, and campgrounds are also available at lakeside. Because the lake levels can fluctuate significantly annually, some ramps may not be usable during low water periods. The fishery is managed under statewide regulations with no exceptions.

Contact: US Army Corps of Engineers, (409) 384-5716; Texas Parks and Wildlife District Office, (409) 384-9572; Jasper Chamber of Commerce, (409) 384-2762

35 Lake Livingston

Description of area: Livingston is an impoundment on one of the major rivers in the eastern half of Texas, the Trinity. It is also one of the largest, spreading out over 90,000 surface acres. Maximum depth is 77 feet and water level fluctuation averages 2 feet per year. Water clarity is usually turbid in the upper sections of the reservoir and moderately so in the remainder of the lake. Vegetation is limited to some native species in the coves and shorelines of the upper sections and non-native water hyacinth is prevalent in many areas. Boathouses and docks also provide cover for gamefish along the shorelines. The reservoir is under the control of the Trinity River Authority.

Major species: White bass, largemouth bass, striped bass, hybrid striped bass, catfish, crappie

Rating of fishery: Catfish, white bass, and crappie are excellent. Largemouth bass and striped bass are good.

The fishing: Livingston is considered to be one of the best white bass and striped bass fisheries in Texas. The white bass make massive spawning runs up the tributaries in late winter and are easy to catch on a wide variety of small lures. During the rest of the year, they can be found around the creek channels, main lake points,

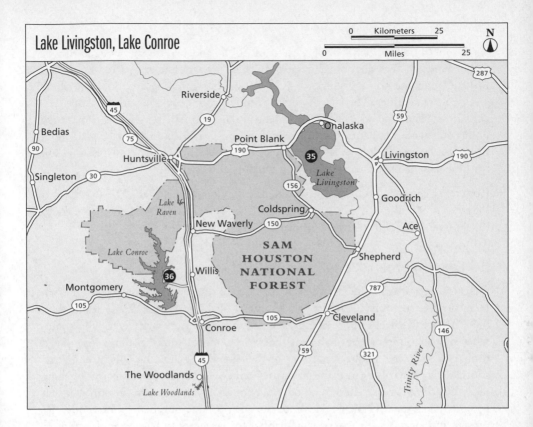

and humps in the lower end of the reservoir. Jigs, spoons, and slabs fished close to the bottom will tease them into reactive strikes. Striped and hybrid striped bass are also plentiful in Livingston. Trolling jigs, vertically jigging spoons, bouncing slabs off the bottom, and drift fishing live bait are productive methods for catching them. From the 190 Bridge south along the river channel, main lake points, and the islands and humps near the dam are prime locations to find them. Largemouth bass fishing is best in the creek arms and coves in the upper sections of the lake where aquatic vegetation is present. Spring and fall are the easiest times of the year to find and catch them. They are in shallower water during those seasons and respond to an assortment of proven lures including spinner baits, top waters, and plastic creature baits. Crappie fishing is most notable in the spring along brushy tributaries in the northern sections of Livingston. Boat docks and brush piles as well as bridge pilings provide excellent cover during the summer and fall. Minnows and small jigs are reliable choices for catching a mess of them. Catfish are thick in Livingston, primarily blue catfish, and they respond well to cut and natural baits. Good places to fish for them are on flats adjacent to creek channels, brush piles, and riprap areas.

Directions: Take US 190 east from Huntsville approximately 25 miles to the town of Point Blank. Turn right on SH 156 and follow to the first intersection where SH 156 turns south. Go through the intersection, heading east to the Point Blank free launching ramp.

Additional information: A wide variety of public and private services catering to anglers and campers surround Livingston. There are 6 public ramps and numerous private launching areas. Livingston State Park offers camping and boat launching and day-use facilities. The lake lies only 50 miles from Houston and gets considerable use during holidays, weekends, and during the summer. The fishery is managed under statewide regulations with one exception: For areas of the lake that lie in Polk, San Jacinto, Trinity, and Walker Counties, the daily bag and possession limit for blue and channel catfish in any combination is 50 fish.

Contact: Livingston–Polk County Chamber of Commerce, (936) 327-4929; Texas Parks and Wildlife District Office, (979) 822-5067; Lake Livingston State Park, (936) 365-2201; Trinity River Authority, (936) 365-2292

36 Lake Conroe (see map on page 83)

Description of area: Lake Conroe is a 20,000-acre reservoir impounded on the San Jacinto River surrounded by the Sam Houston National Forest. Water levels fluctuate from 1 to 3 feet in normal inflow years and the water clarity is usually somewhat stained. Shoreline vegetation is sparse in Conroe. Some standing submerged timber exists in the northern portions of the lake. Fish-attracting habitat along the shoreline is primarily man-made structure including boat docks and private fishing piers and riprap areas. There is an ongoing aquatic habitat restoration project that is reintroducing native plants back into the lake. A large number of brush piles are present in Conroe and these provide habitat for largemouth bass, crappie, sunfish, and catfish. The lake has been heavily stocked since 2002 with largemouth bass and hybrid stripers. Reservoir control is maintained by the San Jacinto River Authority.

Major species: Largemouth bass, catfish, crappie, sunfish, white and hybrid striped bass

Rating of fishery: Catfish, bluegill, and crappie are excellent. Largemouth, white, and hybrid striped bass are good.

The fishing: According to angler surveys, most fishermen come to Conroe to fish for largemouth bass. The lake does produce some large bass as the lake record is over 14 pounds. The bass fishing is limited by the amount of vegetative cover present in the lake but good catches of quality-size bass are common. Most anglers target the man-made structures with spinner baits, jigs, soft-plastic swim baits, and plastic worms. Brush piles are good places to find the larger bass. Spring is the best time to locate willing bass in shallow water, when the bass are spawning. Postspawn, they move to deeper structure. Jigs, spoons, and bottom-crawling plastic worm rigs are what it takes to catch them. Hybrid striped bass introduced in 1995 have added an exciting fishery to Conroe in the open water areas of the southern region. They prowl the creek channels, main lake points, and the dam area.

Popular ways to catch them are trolling jigs or crankbaits, bouncing slabs in white or chartreuse colors off the bottom, or drifting with live shad. In the cool

Weed lines on a secondary point on Lake Conroe are top targets for largemouth bass anglers.

months they will push shad to the surface, offering exciting top-water action. Just about any lure resembling a baitfish will generate strikes. Crappie anglers find action in shallow water during spawning season in the spring. Brush piles and boat docks provide the best cover during most of the year. Timbered areas on the north end also provide habitat for them. Caney Creek, Lewis Creek, and the 1097 Bridge are good areas to find them. Green and red are popular colors for jig fishermen. Minnows are also standard fare for catching them. White bass are eagerly sought during their annual spawning run up tributaries in late winter. They readily smash small, shad-imitating lures fished near the bottom of creeks and holes created by channel bends.

During the summer and fall, they roam the open water creek channels, dropoffs, and main lake points in the southern end of the lake. Vertically jigging small slabs is a proven method for catching them. Catfish are everywhere and it takes little effort to catch a mess of them. Natural or prepared baits drifted or bottom fished will attract them. Baiting an area with soured grain is an excellent way to attract large numbers to a small area quickly. Conroe also has an excellent bluegill fishery. Bluegills 12 inches in length are not uncommon and there are large numbers of these mostly neglected yet tasty panfish available. Red wigglers and crickets fished close to the bottom around brush piles and boat docks are productive methods to entice them.

Directions: Take I-45 north from Conroe approximately 8 miles and turn west on FM 830. Travel 5 miles to the free 2-lane public launch ramp at the end of the road.

Map: DeLorme: Texas Atlas and Gazetteer: Page 71 E11

Additional information: Nine sites around Conroe offer angler-related services. Three of them have camping facilities. The Lake Conroe Convention and Visitors Bureau can supply details on each site. The US Forest Service also provides 2 launch ramps, which require a fee. The fishery at Conroe is subject to statewide regulations except for largemouth bass. Minimum length limit is 16 inches and daily bag limit is 5 bass per person. Also, if a grass carp is caught, it must be quickly released unharmed.

Contact: Texas Parks and Wildlife District Office, (979) 822-5067; Lake Conroe Convention and Visitors Bureau, (877) 4-CONROE; San Jacinto River Authority, (936) 588-1111; US Forest Service, (936) 344-6205

37 Lake Nacogdoches (see map on page 77)

Description of area: It may be small at 2,200 surface acres, but Nacogdoches is known as a trophy bass fishery located on Loco Bayou, 10 miles west of the city of Nacogdoches deep in the pine woods of East Texas. Maximum depth is 40 feet. Water levels fluctuate only 1 to 3 feet in an average rainfall year and the water remains moderately clear year-round. The primary submerged aquatic vegetation is hydrilla. Some standing timber and man-made structures along the shoreline provide additional cover for bass. The city of Nacogdoches is the controlling water authority.

Major species: Largemouth bass, crappie, sunfish

Rating of fishery: Fishing for largemouth bass is excellent. Sunfish is good, while crappie fishing is only fair.

The fishing: Anglers come to Lake Nacogdoches to target the excellent numbers of large bass available in this reservoir. The lake record weighed more than 14 pounds. Late winter and early spring are the best times to catch a double-digit-size largemouth. Bass build nests along the shorelines, the edges of vegetated areas, and around boat docks, making them easier to locate. Lipless crankbaits, spinner baits, and jigs will produce strikes. Fishing over the top of vegetation with a rapid stop-and-go technique is a productive method for pulling bass out of the grass. During the summer bass move to creek channels and main lake points and can be caught on jigs, Carolina-rigged plastic creature baits, and deep-diving crankbaits. In the summer top-water lures fished along the weed beds early and late in the day are also a popular technique for tempting hungry largemouths. Crappie populations are low in this reservoir. Fishing spawning beds during April and May for bluegill and red-ear sunfish is also a popular activity for many anglers on Nacogdoches. Fly-fishing small, dark nymphs or poppers over nests are sure ways to catch a stringer full of them.

Directions: From Nacogdoches, travel west on CR 225 for 8 miles, turn north at the Eastside Park sign, and follow to boat ramp. No fee required.

Map: DeLorme: Texas Atlas and Gazetteer: Page 60 F3

Additional information: Two parks operated by the city of Nacogdoches are located on the southern end of the reservoir. Both have launch ramps, docks, and a picnic and swimming area. No fees are charged to use the facilities. There are no campgrounds available around the lake. The fishery is managed under statewide regulations with one exception: For largemouth bass, only fish 16 inches or less may be retained, except that any bass 24 inches or longer may be placed in a live-well or other aerated holding device, weighed with personal scales, and then immediately released or donated to the ShareLunker Program.

Contact: Texas Parks and Wildlife District Office, (409) 384-9572; city of Nacogdoches, (936) 564-3708; Nacogdoches Convention and Visitors Bureau, (888) 653-3788

38 Lake Pinkston (see map on page 77)

Description of area: Compared to most bass-fishing lakes in Texas, Lake Pinkston, at only 500 surface acres, is a molecule of clear water located on Sandy Creek just west of the city of Center. But don't let its size fool you. Pinkston is a trophy-largemouth-bass fishery with some impressive credentials. It has produced a bass that weighed 16.9 pounds. That fish was a state rod-and-reel record. Maximum depth is 45 feet, water levels fluctuate 1 to 5 feet annually, and the water remains mostly clear year-round. The lake supports reasonable amounts of aquatic vegetation, primarily hydrilla, and has submerged standing timber. The city of Center is the controlling water authority.

Major species: Largemouth bass, crappie, sunfish

Rating of fishery: Largemouth bass fishing is excellent. Crappie and sunfish are good.

The fishing: Anglers come to Pinkston hoping to catch a trophy-sized bass, and the numbers of large fish in this tiny reservoir gives them an excellent opportunity to do so. Spring is the season when most large bass are caught. Spinner baits, top-water lures, and Texas-rigged plastics worked over the nests account for a large number of successful catches. Jigs and Senko-type lures will also take fish when they are spawning. During the summer months fishing the edges of vegetation with top waters and crankbaits early and late in the day are productive methods to generate strikes. Bass will also school in late summer near the dam. Small crankbaits, spoons, and jerk baits are good choices to entice them. Crappie fishing is good on Pinkston. Fishing brushy creek channels and submerged brush piles with jigs or minnows is the best way to get into some serious "perch jerking" as the locals refer to fishing for them. Anglers interested in fishing for large bluegill and red-ear sunfish concentrate their efforts in late spring during their spawning season. Small jigs or flies worked over the beds in shallow water can result in fast and furious action for this delectable species.

Directions: From Center travel approximately 10 miles west on SH 7 to Aiken. Turn north on CR 1211 and continue to Sandy Creek Park on the lake.

Map: DeLorme: Texas Atlas and Gazetteer: Page 60 D6

Additional information: Two boat launch areas are available on Pinkston. One is located on the east end at Sandy Creek Park, the other is on the west end near the dam. Primitive camping facilities are available but there are no other services. No fees are charged for launching or camping. Both areas are operated by the city of Center. The fishery is managed under statewide regulations with these exceptions: A 14- to 21-inch slot limit is in effect for largemouth bass. Only 1 largemouth longer than 21 inches may be kept each day. Also, grass carp are protected and if caught must be released unharmed. Trot lines for catfish are not allowed on Pinkston.

Contact: City of Center, (936) 598-2941; Texas Parks and Wildlife District Office, (409) 384-9572

Hill Country Region

39 Lake Austin (see map on page 90)

Description of area: Lake Austin lies within the city limits of its namesake and covers approximately 1,600 acres. Formed by damming the Colorado River, Austin is primarily a flood-control and electric-power-generating reservoir under control of the Lower Colorado River Authority. Water fluctuation remains minor in an average inflow year and the water remains mostly clear. Aquatic vegetation is plentiful along shorelines, most of it non-native species including water milfoil and hydrilla. Boathouses and fishing docks are abundant along the shorelines, providing additional habitat for gamefish. The lake has a high recreational use on weekends, holidays, and during the summer. This makes fishing during the week and at night popular for anglers who want to avoid the crowds.

Note: Due to low water levels, public launch ramps are closed. Contact local authorities for current updates.

Major species: Largemouth bass, sunfish, catfish

Rating of fishery: Largemouth bass fishing is excellent. Sunfish is good; catfish is fair.

The fishing: Fishing for largemouth bass is the most popular angling activity on Lake Austin. The lake has an excellent population of bass 8 pounds or larger. The lake record for the species is over 14 pounds. It has also produced 7 bass that weighed 13 pounds or more and were entered in Texas Parks and Wildlife's Share-Lunker Program. Primary target areas for bass anglers are the edges of weed beds along shorelines, boat docks, marinas, and the mouths of creeks and small tributaries. Austin is a clear-water lake and that makes bass in shallow water easy to spook. For that reason and because Austin is a high-use recreational lake, many anglers opt for night fishing, especially during the summer months. Buzz baits, spinner baits, and jigs worked along the edges of weed lines and around boat docks at night produce quality bass. Fishing for sunfish is also popular on Lake Austin. Crickets or red wigglers fished off the docks and along the weed-lined drop-offs can result in heavy stringers. Catfish numbers are low in Austin but they can be caught on cut or prepared baits fished along the river channel and around boat docks.

Directions: Lake Austin is located northwest of the center of the city just west of Loop 360. For midlake access, travel south on Loop 360 and cross over the lake on the Pennybacker Bridge. The boat ramp is on the east side of the loop and lies below the bridge. An entrance and launch fee is required.

Map: DeLorme: Texas Atlas and Gazetteer: Page 69 E10

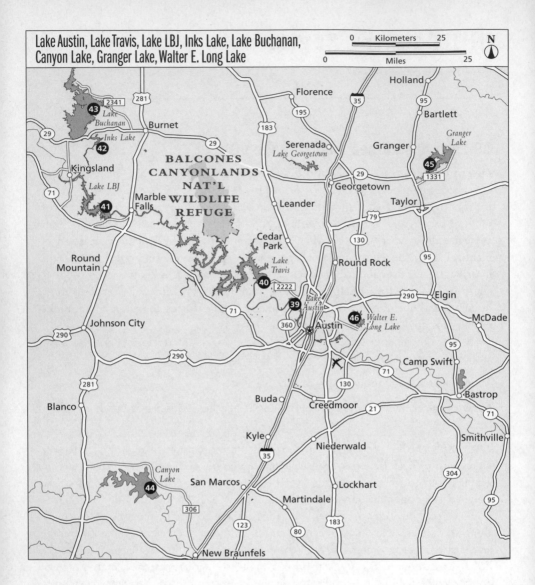

Lake Austin, Lake Travis, Lake LBJ, Inks Lake, Lake Buchanan, Canyon Lake, Granger Lake, Walter E. Long Lake

Additional information: Seven parks are available for public use around the lake. Four of them have launch ramps. Emma Long Park offers camping facilities. Contact the City of Austin Parks and Recreation Department for reservations. Four of the parks are operated by Travis County the other 3 are maintained by the Parks and Recreation Department. Contact them for details. Bank fishermen have access at the Loop 360 Bridge, Emma Long Park, Mary Quinlan Park, and Fritz Hughes Park. The fishery is managed under statewide regulations. The lake contains grass carp for vegetation control. If caught, they must be released immediately unharmed.

Contact: City of Austin Parks and Recreation Department, (512) 499-6700; Texas Parks and Wildlife District Office, (512) 353-0072; Travis County, (512) 854-7275

40 Lake Travis (see map on page 90)

Description of area: Travis is one of a series of narrow high-bluff reservoirs located on the Colorado River northwest of the city of Austin. Maximum surface area is 18,600 acres and the water levels fluctuate widely, between 10 and 20 feet annually. Lower portions of the lake remain mostly clear throughout the year. Upper regions are somewhat turbid. Maximum depth is 190 feet. The lake is mostly devoid of any submerged aquatic vegetation. Boathouses, docks, rock ledges, and boulder piles provide gamefish cover. The Lower Colorado River Authority is the controlling agency.

Note: Due to low water levels, all public ramps are closed as of this writing. Contact the LCRA for current updates.

Major species: Largemouth bass, Guadalupe bass, white bass, striped bass, catfish

Rating of fishery: Largemouth bass, Guadalupe bass, white bass, and catfish are good. Striped bass is fair, and crappie fishing is poor.

The fishing: Lack of aquatic vegetation limits the largemouth bass population on Travis but the lake still provides a good fishery for them. Anglers must learn to fish the rocks and docks with grubs, jigs, drop-shot rigs, and bottom–crawling plastic creature lures in order to score on largemouth on Travis. During the spring spawn, fishing the upper sections along the shorelines is the best time to catch the larger bass. Sight fishing in clear water requires stealth so anglers need to be willing to make longer casts in order not to spook fish off their beds. Spinner baits, jigs, and jerk baits fished over the nests are good choices to generate strikes.

During the rest of the year, concentrate on rock ledges, main lake points, and boat docks. Some large bass are available in Travis, and the lake record for the species is over 14 pounds. Guadalupe bass numbers are good too. They will hit the same lures as the largemouth but downsizing is necessary to catch them. Small tubes, crankbaits, grubs, and jigs fished along the rocky points and ledges are productive tactics. White bass are easiest to locate and catch in late winter when they move up the lake and into tributaries to spawn. Fish will relocate to the mouth of flowing creeks and also up into the Pedernales River. They are easily caught on small jigs, spinners, and crankbaits.

After the spawn they move back down the creeks and locate on main lake points and boulder piles in the lower end of the reservoir. Fishing slabs vertically or trolling small spoons and jigs will catch them. Travis has been stocked regularly with striped bass since 1973. This has produced good fishing opportunities for this remarkable species. The best fishing areas are in the lower end of the reservoir. Trolling white bucktail jigs and large crankbaits over submerged rock piles and main lake points are effective techniques. Vertical bait fishing with live shad is also a proven method for doing battle with stripers on Travis. The lake record for this species is over 30 pounds. Fishing cut bait or prepared baits up the river and around boat docks will take catfish.

Directions: Take the 360 Loop on the west side of Austin to FM 2222. Turn west and follow for approximately 6 miles to RR 620. Turn left and continue for approximately 5 miles to the Mansfield Dam Road. Look for Mansfield Dam Park on the left.

Additional information: There are at least 15 park areas surrounding Lake Travis. The parks are operated by the Lower Colorado River Authority and Travis County Parks and Recreation Department. Contact them for details and maps of the lake area. The fishery is managed under statewide regulations with no exceptions.

Contact: Travis County Parks and Recreation Department, (512) 854-7275; Lower Colorado River Authority, (800) 776-5272; Texas Parks and Wildlife District Office, (512) 353-0072

41 Lake LBJ (see map on page 90)

Description of area: Lake Lyndon Baines Johnson (LBJ) lies just west of the city of Marble Falls on the Colorado River and is part of the chain of water-supply and flood-control lakes known as the Highland Lakes Chain. Maximum surface area is 6,600 acres and depth is 90 feet at the dam. Water levels remain mostly constant annually and the water is fairly clear year-round. The Lower Colorado River Authority is the controlling agency for the reservoir. The upper end of the lake and creeks support a variety of submerged, emerged, and floating plant species. The lower end is mostly rocky shoreline and highly developed with many boat docks and fishing piers providing additional habitat for gamefish.

    Note: Low water levels have forced all public ramps to be closed at press time. Contact the LCRA for current updates.

Major species: Largemouth bass, white bass, crappie, catfish

Rating of fishery: Largemouth bass, white bass, crappie, and catfish are good. Smallmouth bass and Guadalupe bass are fair.

The fishing: LBJ is a clear-water lake surrounded by boat docks, and that is where a large portion of the largemouth bass are caught, on jigs, jerk baits, and Texas-rigged plastic worms. In the spring bass move into the creeks and small inlets to spawn and respond to top-water lures, jerk baits, and jigs. Boat docks on the upper end of the reservoir are also prime locations to find them on their nests. Some bass hot spots include the Ranch Coves area and the confluence of the Llano and Colorado Rivers. During the summer they move to deep-water docks, rocky ledges, and the main lake points near the dam. Crankbaits and jigs are good choices to reach them. In the winter Horseshoe Bay, just west of the Wirtz Dam, is a good place to fish for them. A power plant discharges hot water in the area and the warmth attracts baitfish and bass too.

    Crappie fishing on LBJ can be good. Look for them on the many brush piles placed by anglers along shorelines and main lake points. Docks are also hot spots for crappie, especially those with sunken brush around them. Minnows, jigs, and small spinners with catch them. White bass fishing can be excellent in late winter when they move up the lake into the Colorado and Llano Rivers to spawn. Small jigs, crankbaits, jigs, and spoons fished close to the bottom of the channels will catch them. Bank anglers can fish them from the shoreline at the Kingsland Lions

Club Park located on RR 2900 in the upper end of the reservoir. Late February through March is prime time to find them in the rivers. Fishing for channel catfish is best in the shallow upper river on natural baits and stink baits fished just off the river channel and near brush piles. Guadalupe and smallmouth bass prefer the clear, rocky areas in the lower end of the lake. Fish small crankbaits, drop-shot rigs, jigs, and craw worms on a Texas rig near rocky ledges and points to find them.

Directions: From Marble Falls travel southwest on FM 2147 for approximately 6 miles to the Wirtz Dam Cottonwood ramp. Launching is free.

Map: DeLorme: Texas Atlas and Gazetteer: Page 69 D7

Additional information: There are no camping facilities located around the lake. Call the Marble Falls Chamber for area accommodations. Two parks on the lake offer launch ramps, courtesy docks, and picnic facilities. The free ramp located at the dam is operated by the Lower Colorado River Authority. The other park requires a launch fee and is located on the Llano River arm of the reservoir on the north end of the lake. The fishery is managed under statewide regulations with no exceptions. A free map of the reservoir is available from the Lower Colorado River Authority.

Contact: Lower Colorado River Authority, (512) 473-4083; Marble Falls/Lake LBJ Chamber of Commerce, (830) 693-2815; Texas Parks and Wildlife District Office, (512) 353-0072

42 Inks Lake (see map on page 90)

Description of area: Located on the picturesque Colorado River, Inks Lake, at 861 surface acres, is considered one of the most scenic small reservoirs in Texas. The lake is located just west of the city of Burnet. Water levels fluctuate no more than 1 foot on average and water clarity is excellent. Maximum depth is 60 feet. Little aquatic vegetation is present in the lake. Most gamefish habitat consists of rocky ledges, boulder piles, and boat docks. Some overhanging brush is present in shallower coves. The Lower Colorado River Authority is the controlling agency. Inks Lake State Park is located on the eastern side of the reservoir and is operated by the Texas Parks and Wildlife Department.

Major species: Largemouth bass, Guadalupe bass, white bass, crappie, catfish

Rating of fishery: Largemouth, Guadalupe bass, and sunfish are good. Catfish and white bass are fair.

The fishing: Inks Lake contains good populations of largemouth and Guadalupe bass. For the most part, they receive little pressure from visitors, who primarily come to the park to camp and to fish for sunfish and catfish off the bank. The lake record for largemouth bass is 11.99 pounds, so the fishery has the potential to produce large fish. Crankbaits and jigs worked along the ledges and around the boulder piles will take fish. Spinner baits, jigs, and soft plastic jerk baits fished around and under the boat docks are also good ways to tempt them. Use smaller lures for the

Inks Lake is known for its excellent largemouth bass fishing.

Guadalupe bass. Dark-colored jigs, tube baits, and grubs will get their attention along the rocky points and ledges. White bass move up to the head of the reservoir in late winter to spawn and are stopped by the dam on Lake Buchanan just upriver. They will strike small jigs, spoons, and crankbaits fished in the tailrace. During the summer they can be found on main lake points and boulder piles in the main lake. Small chrome or white slabs fished vertically are a proven method to catch them. Sunfish are plentiful and large in Inks. Crickets, small red wiggler worms, and mealworms are productive baits. Try fishing around deep-water boat docks and over rock piles to find the larger fish. Catfish can be caught from the bank on natural and prepared baits.

Directions: From Burnet travel 9 miles west on SH 29 to Park Road 4. Turn left and follow the road 3 miles to park entrance.

Map: DeLorme: Texas Atlas and Gazetteer: Page 69 B7

Additional information: Inks Lake Park is a very popular destination for campers and anglers so reservations are a good idea. There are no other public facilities around the lake, but angler-related services are available in Burnet and on SH 29 just west of the turnoff for Inks Lake. The fishery is managed under statewide regulations with no exceptions.

Contact: Inks Lake State Park, (512) 793-2223; Lake Buchanan/Inks Lake Chamber of Commerce, (512) 793-2803; Texas Parks and Wildlife District Office, (512) 353-0072

43 Lake Buchanan (see map on page 90)

Description of area: Lake Buchanan spreads across 22,300 acres and lies west of the city of Burnet on the Colorado River. The east side of the lake from the Silver Creek area to the dam is composed of rocky bluffs and boulder-strewn points. The west side is flatter, shallower, and has shoreline brushy cover when the lake is near conservation pool level. Several small islands and underwater humps offer midlake structure. Maximum depth is 132 feet at conservation pool levels. The lower end of the reservoir is generally clear, while the upper end is usually stained year-round. The lake level fluctuates widely depending on annual inflows, and some launch ramps may not be available in late summer. The Lower Colorado River Authority is the controlling agency.

Note: Low water levels have closed all public boat ramps as of press time. Small boats, canoes, and kayaks may be launched from the shore. Call ahead for current conditions.

Major species: Largemouth bass, Guadalupe bass, white bass, striped bass, crappie, catfish

Rating of fishery: Striped bass, white bass, and catfish are excellent. Largemouth bass is good. Crappie is fair.

The fishing: Striped bass are what draw most anglers to Buchanan. Millions of striped bass fingerlings have been stocked during the past 30 years to maintain a robust fishery for these very popular and hard-fighting gamefish. Both white bass and stripers migrate up the lake and into the river in late winter and then move back to the main lake for the summer and fall. Colorado Bend State Park is located on the river above the reservoir and provides excellent wade- and bank-fishing opportunities for catching white bass and stripers when they make their annual spawning run. Favorite techniques used in the lake for catching stripers include trolling bucktail jigs with a white worm trailer, vertically jigging slabs or spoons, and drift fishing with live shad. Smaller lures in the same patterns and fished the same way will also catch white bass.

During the summer and fall, it is possible to find them on the surface chasing shad early in the mornings and late in the evenings. Top-water lures, crankbaits, and swim baits will catch them. When the water heats up, stripers and whites go deep and suspend along the river channel, over underwater rock piles and humps. Fishing live shad close to the bottom or bouncing a slab through them are effective means of generating strikes. Largemouth and Guadalupe bass are also present in good numbers in Buchanan. The upper river remains stained most of the year and largemouth bass stay in shallower water as a result. Top-water lures, spinner baits, buzz baits, and plastic worms are good choices to tempt them. In the clearer water in the south end of the lake, jigs, crankbaits, and drop-shot rigs fished along rock ledges, drop-offs, and boulder piles will produce fish. Use small plastic grubs, finesse worms, and tube jigs for the Guadalupe bass along rock piles, ledges, and main lake points. Catfish are possible all over the lake. Garrett Island and Flag Island are hot spots for catching them on cut bait drifted along the drop-offs and flats.

Sandbars and humps on Lake Buchanan are good places to find striped bass feeding on schools of shad.

Directions: From Burnet take FM 2341 northwest approximately 10 miles. Look for the boat ramp on the left. There is no fee to launch.

Map: *DeLorme: Texas Atlas and Gazetteer:* Page 69 A7

Additional information: Four parks are available around Buchanan: Blackrock, Cedar Point, Canyon of the Eagles, and Colorado Bend, all with camping facilities. Inks Lake State Park is just a few miles south of Buchanan off SH 29 and also has campsites. There are 4 paved boat ramps on the eastern shore, one on the west. Other angler- and camper-related services are available nearby. Contact the Buchanan/Inks Lake Chamber of Commerce for details. The fishery is managed under statewide regulations with no exceptions.

Contact: Lake Buchanan/Inks Lake Chamber of Commerce, (512) 793-2803; Lower Colorado River Authority, (800) 776-5272; Colorado Bend State Park, (325) 628-3240; Texas Parks and Wildlife District Office, (512) 353-0072

44 Canyon Lake (see map on page 90)

Description of area: Canyon is a scenic impoundment located on the Guadalupe River 16 miles north and west of the city of New Braunfels. Surface area at conservation pool level is 8,300 acres. Water levels fluctuate 2 to 5 feet in years with average rainfall. Lower end of the reservoir is clear while the upper end remains somewhat stained. Maximum depth is 125 feet. Very little aquatic vegetation is present in the lake. Gamefish habitat consists of flooded timber, rocky points, chunk rock piles, ledges, and man-made structures along the shoreline. The upper river section has driftwood jams and flooded timber areas. The Army Corps of Engineers is the controlling agency for the reservoir.

Note: Due to low water levels, some public ramps and other facilities are closed as of press time. Check with local authorities for updated information.

Major species: Largemouth bass, smallmouth bass, Guadalupe bass, striped and white bass, catfish

Rating of fishery: Striped bass, white bass, and catfish populations are excellent. Largemouth bass is good. Guadalupe and smallmouth bass are fair.

The fishing: The best largemouth bass fishing is in the upper sections of the lake and in the major coves of the main lake. Turkey Creek and the Cranes Mill area are hot spot areas. Top waters fished early in the morning along the edges of creek channels and lay-downs along shorelines will generate strikes. During the day Wacky-rigged plastic worms and jigs fished in 8 to 10 feet along the points and channels are proven methods. Crankbaits in crawfish patterns worked along rocky points and ledges will take fish too. Guadalupe bass and smallmouth can be caught in the lower lake on rock piles, drop-offs, and along steep bluffs. Small crankbaits, tube baits, grub jigs, and drop-shot rigs are good lure choices. Striped bass fishing is also a major draw for anglers on Canyon. Stripers have been stocked regularly into the lake since 1973 to maintain the fishery. In late winter stripers move up the lake into the mouths of creeks and up the river.

Large top-water lures, bucktail jigs, and live bait are the most consistent producers. Target rock piles, river-bend holes, and cut banks in the river. In the sum-

Rocky shorelines are the rule on scenic Canyon Lake and they provide good fishing areas for many species of gamefish.

mer and fall, trolling jigs, crankbaits, and drifting live bait over the ends of main lake points, creek channels, and rocky ledges in the lower end of the reservoir will catch fish. Comal Park and the hump in front of the dam are hot spots for stripers. White bass follow the same seasonal patterns as do the stripers. Smaller lures in the same patterns and fished in the same areas will produce hookups for these feisty game-fish. Late summer and into fall, stripers and whites will chase shad to the surface, providing exciting top-water lure action. Look for this activity around main lake points and islands. Catfishing is best in the upper end of the lake on prepared and natural baits fished on the flats adjacent to the creek and river channels. Brush piles and timber jams also provide excellent habitat for large blue and flathead catfish.

There is a fish-consumption advisory in effect for Canyon issued by the Texas Department of State Health Services. Adults and children 12 and older are advised to eat no more than two 8-ounce servings per month of striped bass and longnose gar. Children under 12 should eat no more than two 4-ounce servings per month. Pregnant women, women who could become pregnant, and mothers who are breastfeeding are advised not to eat any striped bass or longnose gar from the lake. Mercury levels in these fish are the concern.

Directions: From New Braunfels take FM 306 about 16 miles to Canyon City. Go through town and continue for approximately 2 miles. Turn left at the Jacob's Creek Park sign and then right at Sunchaser Marine. The ramp is on the first road to the left. Boat launching is free.

Map: DeLorme: Texas Atlas and Gazetteer: Page 69 I7

Additional information: Five parks around Canyon offer camping facilities. They are Potters Creek, Cranes Mill, Comal Park, Canyon Park, and Jacob's Park North. The Army Corps of Engineers manages 7 parks around the lake. Others are oper-ated by Comal County and private businesses. Contact the Corps Office and Can-yon Lake Chamber of Commerce for details on services available. The fishery on Canyon is subject to statewide regulations with no exceptions.

Contact: Texas Department of State Health Services, (512) 834-6757; US Army Corps of Engineers, (830) 964-3341; Canyon Lake Chamber of Commerce, (800) 528-2104; Texas Parks and Wildlife Department District Office, (512) 353-0072

45 Granger Lake (see map on page 90)

Description of area: Granger is a 4,000-acre impoundment on the San Gabriel River approximately 10 miles north of the city of Taylor, northeast of Austin. Maximum depth is 50 feet. Water levels fluctuate 2 to 5 feet and the lake clarity varies from moderately turbid to turbid. Aquatic vegetation is minimal to none. Shorelines are brushy and the lake has plenty of stumps and fallen timber. The main lake has a large number of man-made brush piles. The US Army Corps of Engineers is the controlling water body authority.

Major species: Crappie, catfish, white bass, largemouth bass

Rating of fishery: Crappie and catfish are excellent. White bass is good. Largemouth bass is fair to poor.

The fishing: Granger is known for its population of large crappie. The numerous brushy, snag-filled areas in the San Gabriel River mouth and channel and the Willis Creek area provide excellent habitat for the timber-loving crappie. Spring, during their spawning period, is the season to find them in very shallow water. They cannot resist small jigs or minnows fished in front of their noses. Long rods that can reach into small pockets of cover along shorelines are ideal for presenting lures or minnows to fish in very shallow water. During the summer, fall, and winter, the best fishing will be over brush piles scattered throughout the main lake. Use a sonar unit to locate the structure and then fish a small jig or minnow. White bass make an annual run up the tributaries in late winter and will attack just about any small minnow-imitating lure. Favorite choices are spinner jigs, silver spoons, and small crankbaits run close to the bottom of the channels. Summer and fall are when they are most active in the main lake, herding shad to the surface along main lake points and over deep-water creek channels close to the dam. Slabs, small white jigs, and lipless crankbaits are excellent lure choices to catch them. All 3 species of catfish are well represented in Granger. The best areas are the mouths and channels of the tributaries. Logjams, downed trees, and flooded brush are likely hot spots. Cut bait and natural and prepared baits will all take their share of catfish. Largemouth fishing is usually best in the spring in the backs of coves and the shorelines of the main tributaries. Top waters, spinner baits, buzz baits, and jigs are top producers. The Gravel Pit on the south side of the mouth of the San Gabriel River is a hot spot for largemouths.

Directions: From Taylor, travel north on SH 95 to Circleville. Turn right on FM 1331 and head east approximately 6 miles to Taylor Park, located on the left side of the road. Launch fee is required.

Map: DeLorme: Texas Atlas and Gazetteer: Page 69 B12

Additional information: There are 4 parks around Granger operated by the Army Corps of Engineers. Three of them offer camping and picnicking facilities and other conveniences. Contact the Army Corps for details. Bank fishermen can access the San Gabriel River above Granger Lake off of CR 348. The river in this area is popular among anglers who want to fish for white bass during their annual spawning run in late winter.

Contact: US Army Corps of Engineers, (512) 859-2668; Taylor Chamber of Commerce, (512) 352-6364; Texas Parks and Wildlife Department District Office, (512) 353-0072

46 Walter E. Long Lake (see map on page 90)

Description of area: This small power-plant-cooling reservoir is located about 10 miles east of Austin and covers 1,270 acres. Water levels remain fairly constant year-round and water clarity is good. Maximum depth is 60 feet. The lake contains an abundance of native and exotic aquatic plants, which provides ideal largemouth bass habitat. The city of Austin is the controlling authority.

Major species: Largemouth bass, hybrid striped bass, catfish

Rating of fishery: Largemouth bass is excellent. Hybrid striped bass and catfish are good.

The fishing: Since 1979, more than 3 million largemouth bass have been stocked into the lake and the results, from a bass fisherman's viewpoint, are excellent. Large numbers of bass weighing more than 7 pounds are caught regularly. The abundant shoreline vegetation and beds of submerged aquatic plants provide good habitat for largemouth bass. Fishing top-water lures, spinner baits, and weightless plastic worms along the shoreline vegetation will produce good strikes. Working jigs, crankbaits, and jerk baits along the edges of submerged weed beds is also a popular tactic. The water remains warm during the winter when the power plant is generating and this allows bass fishing in shallow water to remain productive year-round. A very good hybrid striped bass fishery is also present in this lake. Look for them on humps, along creek channels, around main lake points, and near the dam. Top-producing lures include bucktail jigs, slabs, and swim baits. Drifting live shad or small sunfish over deep water is a very effective means of catching them during the summer. In the fall and winter, they will school and chase shad to the surface, providing exciting top-water action. Lipless crankbaits, swim baits, and slabs are productive lures to throw at them. Catfish will respond to natural and prepared baits fished on the bottom. Drifting cut bait along creek channels and humps is also a very good method to catch them when they are on the prowl.

Directions: Only one access point to Walter E. Long is available to the public. From the east side of Austin on US 183, take FM 969 east to FM 973. Turn northeast and travel approximately 1 mile to Decker Lake Road. Continue for about 0.5 mile and turn right onto the park road. A park entry fee is required.

Map: DeLorme: Texas Atlas and Gazetteer: Page 69 F12

Additional information: There are no camping facilities at this reservoir. The park is limited to day use only. The fishery is managed under statewide regulations with an exception for largemouth bass. The length limit for largemouth bass is a 14- to 21-inch slot. Bass between 14 and 21 inches must be immediately released. Bass less than 14 inches may be kept. One bass longer than 21 inches may be kept daily. Anglers are encouraged to keep the smaller fish to improve the number of larger bass available.

Contact: City of Austin, (512) 926-5230; Texas Parks and Wildlife Department District Office, (512) 353-0072

47 Brady Creek Reservoir

Description of area: Brady Creek is a 2,000-acre water-supply reservoir located in the north-central section of the Hill County region of central Texas. Maximum

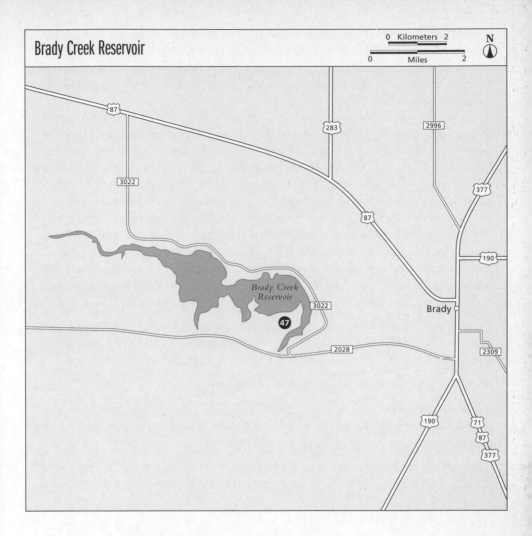

Brady Creek Reservoir

0 Kilometers 2

0 Miles 2

N

3022

87

283

2996

377

3022

87

190

Brady Creek
Reservoir

47

3022

Brady

2028

2309

190

71

87

377

depth is 48 feet and average water level fluctuation is 3 to 5 feet. The water clarity is somewhat stained year-round. As is typical of lakes in this region, aquatic vegetation is scarce. Cover for gamefish is limited to rocky shorelines, ledges, boulder piles, and man-made structures along the shoreline and dead timber. The main tributary is Brady Creek. The city of Brady is the controlling water body authority.

Major species: Largemouth bass, catfish, crappie, white bass

Rating of fishery: Fishing for largemouth bass, catfish, and crappie is good. White bass fishing is fair.

The fishing: Spawning season is the best time of the year to target largemouth bass, crappie, and white bass on Brady. Largemouth bass start moving shallow in February until April. Crappie relocate to shoreline areas with cover in April and May in an average year. Spinner baits, top waters, jerk baits, and jigs as well as plastic creature baits are good choices to tempt the largemouth bass during this period. Look for them in the backs of coves with cover, up the river, and along shorelines with structure in shallow water. During the summer fishing ledges, rock piles, and creek channels with jigs, Carolina-rigged plastic worms, or deep-diving crankbaits will generate strikes.

The lake record for the species is 12.95 pounds. Crappie anglers do best in spring along downed timber, boat docks, and shallow rock piles and any woody cover in the tributaries. Small jigs and minnows are the best producers for generating strikes. White bass will run up Brady Creek starting in late winter after enough rainfall gets the creek flowing. Small spinners, jigs, and crankbaits in shad colors fished close to the bottom of the creek channel, around timber jams, and in pockets or holes along the bank will catch them. Catfish will move into the creek after significant rains and can be readily caught on a variety of natural and prepared baits. Fishing for them around logjams, boulder piles, and boat docks can also be productive. There is a small but catchable population of smallmouth bass in this lake. Main lake points, rock piles, and bluff ledges on the main lake provides habitat. Small jigs, drop-shot rigs, and crankbaits are good choices to catch them.

Directions: From Brady, travel west on FM 2028 for approximately 5 miles and turn right on FM 3022. Follow to Brady City Park, located near the dam. Launching is free.

Map: DeLorme: Texas Atlas and Gazetteer: Page 56 J1

Additional information: The city of Brady maintains 1 park on the lake. Camping facilities are available. Contact the city for details. The fishery is managed under statewide regulations with no exceptions.

Contact: Brady Chamber of Commerce, (325) 597-3491; city of Brady, (325) 597-2152; Texas Parks and Wildlife District Office, (210) 348-6355

Gulf Coast Region

48 Coleto Creek Reservoir

Description of area: Coleto Creek is a 3,100-acre power-plant-cooling reservoir located 15 miles southwest of Victoria, just off US 59. Maximum depth is 46 feet. Water levels fluctuate 1 to 3 feet annually and water clarity is slightly stained to clear. Native and exotic aquatic vegetation is scattered in pockets along the shorelines and in the creeks. The reservoir is fed by 4 tributaries providing good cover for largemouth bass and crappie. Shallow flats, brushy areas, creek channels and ledges, humps, and long, sloping points provide additional habitat.

Major species: Largemouth bass, crappie, catfish, white and hybrid striped bass

Rating of fishery: Largemouth bass and crappie are excellent. Catfish is good. White bass and hybrid striped bass are fair.

The fishing: Largemouth bass and crappie are what draw most anglers to Coleto. Bass weighing 5 to 8 pounds are common and the lake's irregular shoreline offers many places to fish for them. Spring is when bass move to shallow water and are most vulnerable to anglers. Typical bass lures including spinner baits, buzz baits, jerk baits, and plastic creature baits account for a lot of the bass caught from Coleto. Eagle's Nest Cove and Alligator Cove are spring hot spots. When bass move deeper after spawning, jigs, crankbaits, and drop-shot rigs fished on main lake structure, along creek channels and humps, and the edges of weed beds will generate strikes. Road Bed Cove and Ledbetter Point are hot spots. Crappie anglers will want to concentrate on shallow, brushy areas in the creeks during the spring spawn. After completing their reproductive rites, crappie will move to the creek channels and timbered areas in water 12 to 25 feet in depth. The Coletoville and Fannin Bridges are hot spots. Small jigs or minnows are sure producers for the light-biting crappie. Catfishing is excellent along the creek channels, shallow brushy flats, in the mouths of coves, and around the hot water discharge area of the power plant. Cut shad or sunfish is hard to beat as bait for channel and blue catfish. A modest fishery exists for white and hybrid striped bass. Small shad-imitating crankbaits, slabs, and live shad fished over the humps and the ends of main lake points should get their attention. During the cold months the hot water discharge is a good place to find them. The lake was also stocked with 25,000 red-drum fingerlings in 2001, and it is possible some of those fish are still in the lake. Drifting live or cut bait along the drop-offs and humps has been a proven method of hooking up with them.

Directions: From Victoria, travel southwest on US 59 15 miles and look for the Coleto Creek Reservoir access road. Turn right and follow for 1 mile to park entrance. An entrance fee is required.

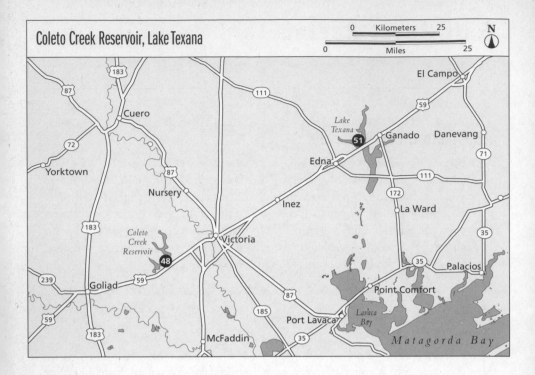

Coleto Creek Reservoir, Lake Texana

Map: DeLorme: Texas Atlas and Gazetteer: Page 79 H8

Additional information: The only access to the lake is through Coleto Creek Park and it is operated by the Guadalupe-Blanco River Authority. The park offers 54 RV sites and other angler- and camper-related services. Call the park for details. The fishery is managed under statewide regulations with an exception for red drum. The daily bag limit for this species is 3 fish, which must be 20 inches or longer to retain. There is no maximum size limit.

Contact: Guadalupe-Blanco River Authority, (361) 575-6366; Texas Parks and Wildlife District Office, (361) 547-9712; Victoria Chamber of Commerce, (361) 573-5277

49 Lake Corpus Christi

Description of area: Lake Corpus Christi is an 18,300-acre impoundment located on the Nueces River, approximately 20 miles northeast of the city of Corpus Christi. Maximum depth at conservation pool is 60 feet. Water levels can fluctuate widely, as much as 10 to 15 feet annually. Water clarity is usually somewhat stained in the upper regions, fairly clear in the lower main lake. Aquatic vegetation consists of native and exotic species and is abundant in most shallow areas of the lake, providing excellent habitat for largemouth bass and crappie. Other habitat available consists of submerged timber, old road beds, and extended points and underwater islands. The city of Corpus Christi is the controlling authority.

Major species: Largemouth bass, crappie, white bass, catfish

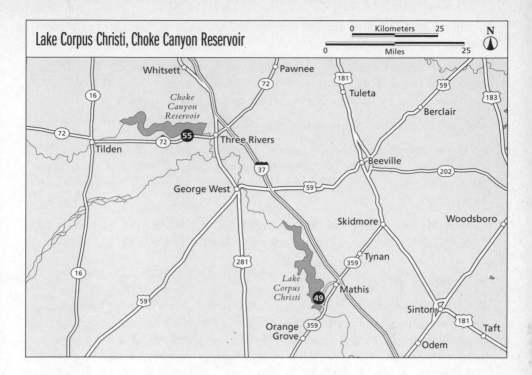

Lake Corpus Christi, Choke Canyon Reservoir

Rating of fishery: Catfish is excellent. Largemouth bass, crappie, and white bass are very good.

The fishing: Bass anglers target the multiple creeks with vegetation on Corpus with top-water lures, spinner baits, jerk baits, and Texas-rigged plastic worms and lip-less crankbaits with great success. Corpus is not noted for its population of large bass but has an excellent population of medium-size fish over 5 pounds. Fishing crankbaits, jigs, and drop-shot rigs along the creek channels and main lake points in the summer and fall are favorite tactics for hooking up with fish. Top-water lures and buzz baits fished along the edges of weed beds early and late in the day are also popular tactics. Try flipping unweighted plastic worms around flooded brush and open pockets of vegetation.

The islands located on the north side of the midlake region are a hot spot for this tactic. Barbon Creek and Pernitas Creek in the southeast corner of the reservoir are also hot spots for bass on Corpus. Crappie anglers do well in the spring around flooded brush and timber in the upper sections of the reservoir and up the Nueces River. Small jigs and minnows are the best bait choices. Fishing around the boat docks and the lighted piers at night is also a popular tactic for catching crappie on Corpus. White bass are easiest to catch in late winter when they make their spawning run into the mouth of the river. Small crankbaits, spinners, and spoons worked along the edges of sandbars and drop-offs along the main channel will entice them. In the summer they can be found along main lake points and underwater humps and the river channel near the dam. Slabs and live shad fished close to the bottom will catch them. Catfish are abundant and can be caught on cut bait and prepared bait throughout the reservoir. The railroad bridge on the west end of the lake is a hot spot for catfish.

Directions: From Corpus Christi take I-37 north for approximately 20 miles to Mathis and take FM 1068 west for 2 miles to Lake Corpus Christi State Park. A small per-person entrance fee is required for ages 13 years and older.

Map: DeLorme: Texas Atlas and Gazetteer: Page 84 B3

Additional information: There are 6 parks located around the lake that offer camping and other angler-related services. Contact the Mathis Chamber of Commerce for details on those facilities. The fishery is managed under statewide regulations with no exceptions.

Contact: Mathis Chamber of Commerce, (361) 547-0177; Lake Corpus Christi State Park, (361) 547-2635; Texas Parks and Wildlife District Office, (361) 547-9712

50 Lake Houston

Description of area: Lake Houston is a 12,000-acre reservoir 15 miles northeast of the city of Houston on the west fork of the San Jacinto River. Maximum depth is 45 feet and the water fluctuates very little in an average rainfall year. The water remains moderately stained year-round. Most of the aquatic vegetation found in the lake is in the east and west forks of the San Jacinto River. The main lake is generally devoid of cover or structure except for pilings on the FM 1960 bridge and the railroad bridge located at midlake. The City of Houston Public Works is the controlling agency for the lake.

Major species: Catfish, crappie, white bass, largemouth bass

Rating of fishery: Catfish and white bass are good. Largemouth bass and crappie are fair.

The fishing: This lake provides excellent opportunities for catching blue and channel catfish. They are the most dominant species. The forks of the rivers are the best locations to fish for them. Cut bait or prepared stink baits fished on the flats adjacent to or in the channels of the rivers are proven tactics. The bridges are also hot spots for them. Drifting cut bait over main lake points is a proven method. Crappie fishing is best in spring in the rivers near flooded brush. Luse Bayou is a hot spot in the spring. The railroad bridge is another excellent location to find them after they spawn. Small minnows and jigs are the best baits. White bass make an annual run up the rivers in late winter and are very responsive to small spinners, crankbaits, and jigs fished along the channel edges and in holes and eddies of the river. During the summer look for them feeding on the surface early and late in the day near the dam.

Directions: Drive north on US 59 from Houston to Humble. Turn east on FM 1960 and drive for approximately 12 miles. Cross the lake. Turn left on the first road and continue to Lake Houston Marina. Launch fee required.

Map: DeLorme: Texas Atlas and Gazetteer: Page 72 G1

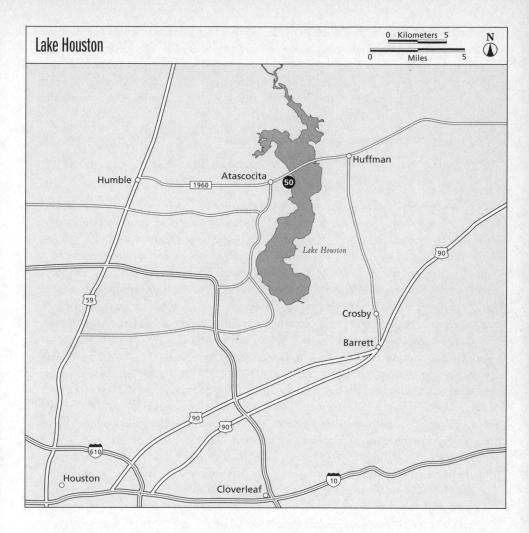

0 Kilometers 5

0 Miles 5

N

Huffman

Humble

1960

Atascocita

50

Lake Houston

90

Crosby

Barrett

59

90

90

610

Houston

Cloverleaf

10

Additional information: Four areas around the lake offer angler- and camping-related facilities. They are BJ's Marina, Camp Paradise, Lake Houston Marina, and Duessen Park. Contact the Humble Chamber of Commerce for details. Fishing is managed under statewide regulations with no exceptions. This lake gets much recreational use during the summer and on holidays and weekends. Best fishing opportunities are during the week.

Contact: Humble Area Chamber of Commerce, (281) 446-2128; Texas Parks and Wildlife District Office, (979) 822-5067; Houston Lake Patrol, (281) 324-2250

51 Lake Texana (see map on page 104)

Description of area: Texana is a 9,700-acre water-supply reservoir located about midway between Corpus Christi and Houston. Maximum depth is 58 feet and water levels can fluctuate between 10 to 15 feet annually. Water clarity is usually stained. Large areas of the lake are covered with water hyacinth. There is abundant submerged native vegetation in some areas that provides good cover for largemouth bass and crappie. The main lake has flooded timber and stump fields that also provide habitat for gamefish. The Navidad River and Sandy Creek are the 2 main tributaries. The Lavaca-Navidad River Authority is the controlling agency for the reservoir.

Major species: Largemouth bass, crappie, catfish, white and hybrid striped bass

Rating of fishery: Crappie is excellent, catfish and white bass are good, largemouth bass and hybrid striped bass are fair.

The fishing: Texana is known as a very good lake to catch a mess of crappie and catfish. The shallow timber and vegetated shorelines are prime spots to target crappie during their spring spawn. Flooded brush in the main tributaries will be holding fish when they move shallow to reproduce. Small minnows and contrasting-colored jigs are good attractors. During the warm months target the timbered creek channels and brush piles in deeper water. The edges of weed beds are good spots to find them too. Catfish are abundant and present all over the reservoir. The mouths of creek channels are excellent areas to find them, especially during an inflow of freshwater. Prepared baits, cut bait, and live bait are all top producers of good catches. Largemouth bass fishing is improving in Texana. Approximately 1 million largemouth bass fingerlings were stocked in the lake in 2006–2007. Those fish should boost the existing population and provide excellent fishing opportunities in the coming years. The Navidad River and adjacent shallow flats known locally as the "jungle" provide a large area of snags and vegetation that translates into excellent bass habitat. Spinner baits, top-water lures, jigs, and plastic worms are favored bass catchers. Fishing the edges of weed beds with jigs, tube baits, and crankbaits is another good tactic for locating largemouths. White bass make a late-winter spawning run up the major tributaries and are easy to catch on small crankbaits, jigs, and spoons. During the hot months look for them in deep water along the creek channels and near the dam. Slabs or jigs worked through suspended schools will usually entice them to bite. Hybrid striped bass locate in the same areas and are often caught using the same tactics.

Directions: From Edna, travel northeast on US 59 approximately 6 miles to the Navidad River public boat launch. There is no fee for launching a boat.

Map: DeLorme: Texas Atlas and Gazetteer: Page 79 F11

Additional information: The Lavaca-Navidad River Authority maintains 6 areas around the lake with boat ramps that are free to use. The LNRA also maintains the Brackenridge Plantation Recreational Area, which offers overnight campsites and other angler amenities. Call the LNRA for details. Texas Parks and Wildlife Department maintains Lake Texana State Park, which also offers overnight camping and fishing facilities. Call the park for information. The fishery is managed under statewide regulations with no exceptions.

Contact: Lavaca-Navidad River Authority, (361) 782-5229; Texana State Park, (361) 782-5718; Texas Parks and Wildlife District Office, (361) 547-9712

South Texas Plains Region

52 Lake Braunig (see map on page 110)

Description of area: Braunig is a power-plant-cooling reservoir of 1,350 acres located approximately 17 miles south of San Antonio just off I-37. Maximum depth is 50 feet and the water level fluctuates 1 to 2 feet annually. Water clarity is usually stained. Calaveras and Chupaderas Creeks are the main tributaries. Vegetation is limited to the shoreline areas and consists mostly of cattails and bulrushes. Main lake cover is limited to riprap areas along the dam, rock jetties, and points of land jutting into the lake. The San Antonio River Authority is the controlling agency.

Major species: Red drum, catfish, hybrid striped bass, largemouth bass

Rating of fishery: Red drum and hybrid striped bass fishing is excellent, catfish is good, and largemouth bass is fair.

The fishing: Braunig offers inland anglers excellent opportunities to tangle with red drum weighing 20 pounds or more. The lake record for the species is 30 pounds. Starting in the early 1990s, the lake has been heavily stocked on an annual basis with red-drum fingerlings. Drifting live shad, sunfish, or tilapia cut bait along the riprap areas and the hot water discharges is a favored means of catching them. They will also hit lures. Lipless crankbaits, spoons, deep-diving crankbaits, and large jigs will catch them. Sometimes they will push baitfish to the surface and feed on them. This behavior provides some top-water fishing opportunities. Look for fish-eating birds diving to the surface to help pinpoint this type of behavior. Spoons or crankbaits are good lure choices to elicit strikes. Braunig is also an excellent lake to hook up with hybrid striped bass. These hard-fighting fish are somewhat similar in habits to the red drum and can be caught in the same areas using similar tackle. They prefer the deeper areas near the dam; riprap areas and the creek channels during the warm months. During the winter the hot water discharge areas attract them. Trolling jigs, large crankbaits, and drifting live or cut bait in deeper areas will also take fish. Largemouth bass fishing is best in late winter to early spring during their spawning period. Spinner baits and plastic creature baits fished along shoreline vegetation will generate strikes from nesting bass. Crankbaits and tube jigs worked along the riprap areas in spring will also take fish. Catfishing is good all over the lake on cut and prepared baits. The jetty and discharge areas and the creek channels are good locations to fish for them.

Directions: From San Antonio take I-37 south for approximately 17 miles. Take exit 130 to the San Antonio River Authority Park.

Map: DeLorme: Texas Atlas and Gazetteer: Page 78 D1

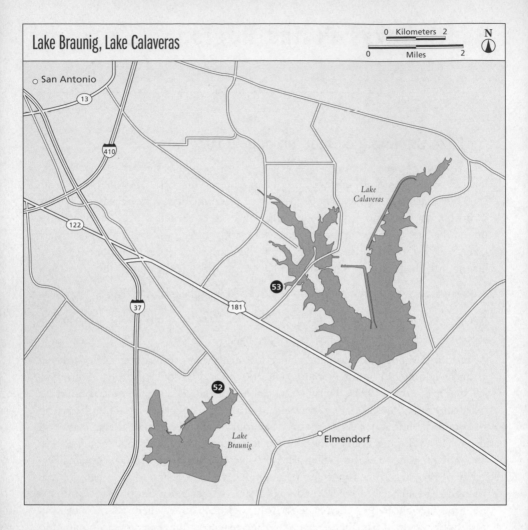

Lake Braunig, Lake Calaveras

0 Kilometers 2
0 Miles 2

N

San Antonio

13

410

122

37

181

122

53

52

Lake Calaveras

Lake Braunig

Elmendorf

Additional information: There are small day-use fees per adult and boat launch. The SARA Park is the only public access and offers primitive camping with no hookups. Call the park for additional information. Fishing licenses are sold at the park entrance. For area lodging call the San Antonio Convention and Visitors Bureau. The fishery is managed under statewide regulations with 2 exceptions: Largemouth bass must be 18 inches or longer to be retained, and red drum have a minimum length requirement of 20 inches with no maximum length, and the daily bag limit is 3 fish per person.

Contact: San Antonio River Authority Park, (210) 635-8289; San Antonio Convention and Visitors Bureau, (800) 447-3372; Texas Parks and Wildlife District Office, (210) 348-6355

53 Lake Calaveras (see map on page 110)

Description of area: Calaveras is another power-plant-cooling reservoir operated by the San Antonio River Authority, located approximately 20 miles southeast of the city of San Antonio. Surface area is 3,600 acres and maximum depth is 45 feet. Water fluctuation is minimal at 1 to 2 feet annually and water clarity remains moderately stained. The main tributaries are Calaveras Creek, Hondo Creek, and Chupaderas Creek. Gamefish habitat consists of shoreline vegetation, riprap areas, and other man-made structures associated with the power plant.

Major species: Red drum, catfish, hybrid striped bass, largemouth bass

Rating of fishery: Red drum, hybrid striped bass, and catfish are excellent. Largemouth bass is fair.

The fishing: Sight-casting for surface-feeding redfish along the intake area is where the hot action is on Calaveras in the summer. If fish are not active on the surface, switch to a cast-and-count technique. Experiment with depth until a fish is caught. Make sure to let the lure free-fall vertically by keeping the reel out of gear and feeding line until the proper depth is achieved. Use a pump-and-drop retrieve. Feather jigs, Kastmaster slabs, and swim baits are good lure choices. Best colors are white, pearl, green, and yellow. The Crappie Wall area on the west side of the reservoir is another hot spot for redfish. Bank-fishing opportunities are available in this area too. Shad or tilapia used as cut or live bait is an excellent means of getting into some hungry redfish on Calaveras. Fishing bait on the bottom or drifting it along the riprap and the warmwater discharge area are effective techniques also. Hybrid stripers like to hang out on the main lake points, the creek channels, and along the dam area. Drifting live shad or sunfish over these areas is usually an excellent means of hooking up with them. Trolling spoons, jigs, and crankbaits will also take fish. Striper Ridge and the West Hump area are hot spots for them. Largemouth bass fishing is best in spring and early summer. Vegetated shoreline areas, the riprap, and man-made structure along the shorelines are good places to find them during this period. The North Reed Beds and Oak Tree Cove areas are hot spots. Catfish are abundant and prevalent all over the lake. Natural and prepared baits are the usual fare for enticing them. The railroad bridge and Picnic Table Cove are hot spot areas. Spring to early summer is prime time to find them roaming the shallow areas.

Directions: From San Antonio travel southeast on US 181 for approximately 20 miles to FM 1604. Turn northeast and follow it to the park entrance on the left.

Map: DeLorme: Texas Atlas and Gazetteer: Page 78 D1

Additional information: The San Antonio River Authority Park on the southeastern side of the reservoir is the only public access to Calaveras. Park entrance and use of facilities requires modest fees. The park is open year-round. Call for details. Area information is available from the San Antonio Convention and Visitors Bureau. The fishery is managed under statewide regulations with 2 exceptions: The minimum

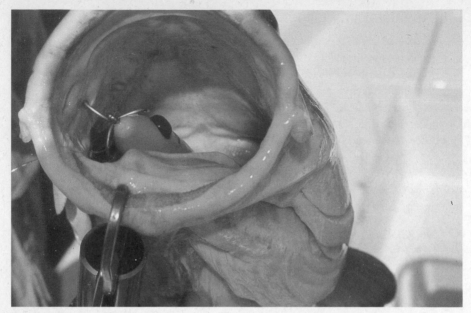

Redfish like this one are not shy about hitting top-water lures on Lake Calaveras.

length limit for largemouth bass is 18 inches, and red drum must be at least 20 inches in length with no maximum length limit and a daily bag limit of 3 fish per person.

Contact: San Antonio River Authority Park, (210) 635-8359; San Antonio Convention and Visitors Bureau, (800) 447-3372; Texas Parks and Wildlife District Office, (210) 348-6355

54 Lake Casa Blanca

Description of area: Casa Blanca is a water-supply reservoir of 1,700 acres located northeast of Laredo. Texas Parks and Wildlife maintains a state park encompassing the southern third of the lake. Maximum depth is 36 feet. Water levels can fluctuate as much as 25 feet in low rainfall years and the water clarity is usually somewhat turbid. The reservoir is under the authority of Webb County. Gamefish habitat consists of shoreline vegetation including cattails and bulrushes. Riprap areas near the dam and flooded timber in the shallow upper end also provide cover for fish. Chacon and San Ygnacio Creeks are the main tributaries.

Major species: Largemouth bass, hybrid striped bass, crappie, catfish

Rating of fishery: Catfish and hybrid striped bass are excellent. Largemouth bass and crappie are good.

The fishing: Casa Blanca has produced some giant largemouth bass in excess of 14 pounds. Most bass range from 3 to 8 pounds. The best fishing for them is late winter to early spring when they are spawning in shallow water. Soft-plastic worms, spin-

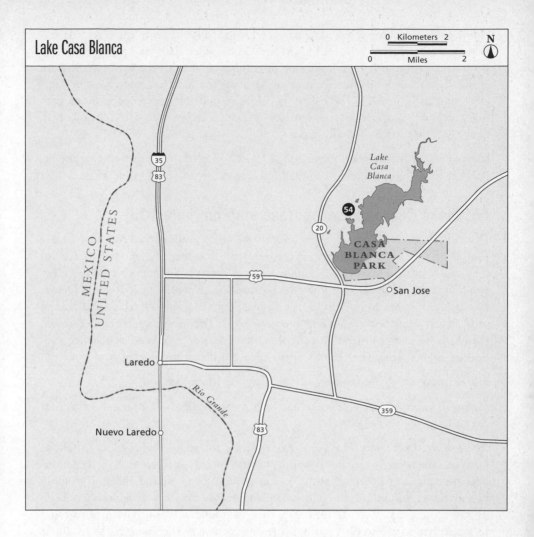

ner baits, and top waters are good lure choices during this period. Lures worked along the vegetated shorelines and the riprap areas will produce strikes. Crappie fishing is good around the flooded timber, the riprap areas, and reed beds in spring and early summer. Hybrid striped bass congregate along main lake points, the dam, and the creek channels. Fishing live shad or small sunfish vertically over deep-water structure is an excellent means of catching them in the spring and summer. In the fall and winter, they will push shad to the surface and that behavior provides exciting top-water action. Small top waters, lipless crankbaits, and slabs will get their attention. Catfish are abundant and can be caught along the timbered channels, the riprap areas, and main lake points on cut or prepared baits fished on the bottom.

Directions: From Laredo head east on US 59 to Loop 20 and drive north to Casa Blanca State Park, located just east of the airport.

Map: DeLorme: Texas Atlas and Gazetteer: Page 83 H7

Additional information: The state park offers the only access to the lake. There is a small per-person entrance fee for visitors 13 and older. This lake is subject to low water levels at certain times of the year, so it is best to contact the park office before going. Casa Blanca was heavily stocked with largemouth bass fingerlings in 2003, 2004, and again in 2011. The fishery is managed under statewide regulations with one exception: Largemouth bass must be at least 18 inches in length to be retained. Daily bag limit is 5 bass of any species.

Contact: Casa Blanca State Park, (956) 725-3826; Laredo Chamber of Commerce, (800) 292-2122; Texas Parks and Wildlife District Office, (210) 348-6355

55 Choke Canyon Reservoir (see map on page 105)

Description of area: Located approximately 60 miles south of San Antonio, Choke Canyon is a 25,700-acre water-supply reservoir for the city of Corpus Christi impounded on the Frio River. Maximum depth is 95 feet and water clarity in the upper end is somewhat stained. The lower lake remains mostly clear year-round. Fluctuation levels can range from 10 to 15 feet. Choke is rich in gamefish habitat. Native and some exotic vegetation are abundant in most areas. The main lake has numerous old road beds, submerged islands, brushy flats, numerous coves and creek channels, and flooded timber areas. The city of Corpus Christi is the controlling agency.

Major species: Largemouth bass, catfish, crappie, white bass

Rating of fishery: Largemouth bass and catfish are excellent. Crappie and white bass are good.

The fishing: Largemouth bass are the top draw for anglers who come to Choke Canyon. The lake has vast areas of prime habitat and a long warm season. Bass numbers are high and fish grow fast thanks to a good forage base and a plentiful supply of aquatic vegetation. It is not unusual for anglers to catch bass weighing 10 pounds or more, and the lake record for bass is over 14 pounds. As is usual for this species in Texas, late winter to early spring, when they move to shallow areas to spawn, is the best time to tangle with big bass. Soft-plastic creature baits, spinner baits, grubs, jigs, and top-water lures are all effective. When water temperatures heat up, bass will retreat to creek channels, humps, main lake points, and submerged weed beds for cover. Jigs, Carolina rigs, deep-diving crankbaits, and drop-shot rigs are good choices for tempting them. Elm Creek, Four Fingers, and Huisache Island are hot spot areas for finding them.

White bass provide exciting fishing in late winter when they move up the Frio River to spawn. Small shad-imitating lures fished on the bottom and in eddies and pools will catch them. During the summer and fall, they move to main lake points, the Frio channel, and the dam area. Trolling spoons, jigs, or vertically presenting live shad or minnows are the usual means of catching them. Catfish are prolific in Choke and can easily be caught on stink baits, cut bait, and cheese baits fished in the creek and river channels and the brushy flats. Crappie are most easily located in the spring in shallow brushy areas and along creek channels with flooded timber. Small jigs and minnows are the best bet to entice them. The Three Fingers shoreline, the SH 99 Bridge, and the Dam Intake area are hot spots to find them.

Directions: From San Antonio travel south on I-37 approximately 60 miles to Three Rivers. Turn west on SH 72 and follow for 4 miles to the South Shore Unit of Choke Canyon State Park, operated by Texas Parks and Wildlife Department.

Map: DeLorme: Texas Atlas and Gazetteer: Page 78 J1

Additional information: TPWD maintains a north unit and south unit of the park as well as 3 other boat-launching areas around Choke Canyon. The north unit of the park offers overnight camping and other angler- and camping-related services. Call the park for details. The fishery is managed under statewide regulations with no exceptions.

Contact: Choke Canyon State Park, (361) 786-3538; city of Corpus Christi, (512) 880-3000; Texas Parks and Wildlife District Office, (361) 547-9712

56 Falcon International Reservoir (see map on page 116)

Description of area: Falcon is a border reservoir shared with Mexico and is located on the Rio Grande about 40 miles east of Laredo. Surface area at conservation pool is 84,000 acres and maximum depth is 110 feet. The upper end remains mostly turbid while the lower main lake is somewhat stained. Water levels can fluctuate widely as the area is basically arid. The lake has minimal aquatic vegetation and is fairly shallow except for the lower end of the main body of water. The International Boundary Commission is the controlling agency.

Major species: Largemouth bass, catfish, crappie, white bass

Rating of fishery: Largemouth bass and catfish are excellent. Crappie and white bass are fair.

The fishing: Falcon is well known among serious bass anglers as a premier lake for catching large numbers of big bass. Big in the context that fish over 7 pounds are plentiful. When the lake is at or close to full, thousands of acres of prime habitat are available and it seems as though there are bass under each bush or tree. Spinner baits, top-water lures, and plastic worms are some of the most productive lures used to locate them. Spring, fall, and winter are the best seasons to fish for largemouth bass on Falcon. The summer is very hot and productive fishing is best at night or early mornings. The lake shoreline is very irregular with lots of timbered points, inlets, and brush-covered flats providing excellent habitat. Rock piles, submerged timber, and flooded man-made structures provide main lake habitat. The lake record for the species is over 15 pounds. Catfish are available all over the lake, and fishing cut, stink, or natural baits along the creek channels, main and secondary points, and shallow brushy flats will produce limits. Crappie and white bass populations are recovering from the drought years. Timbered creeks and brushy points are good places to find them. During the summer main lake humps and rock piles are good places to find the white bass and crappie.

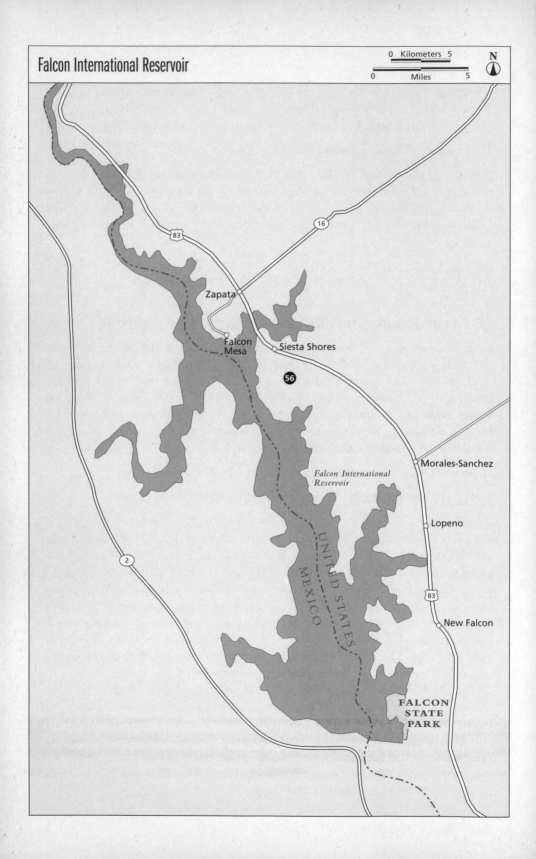

Falcon International Reservoir

Directions: From Laredo, travel southeast on US 83 to Zapata. Look for the Zapata County launch ramp exit located approximately 1 mile southeast of the Arroyo Veleno Bridge. Exit right and continue to the free boat launch ramp.

Map: DeLorme: Texas Atlas and Gazetteer: Page 87 D8

Additional information: Falcon State Park is operated by Texas Parks and Wildlife and is located in the southeastern section of Falcon near the International Dam. The park offers camping, day-use, and boat-launching facilities. Call the park for details and water levels. The city of Zapata has motels, restaurants, guide services, and other angler-related services. Call the Zapata Chamber of Commerce for details. The fishery on the Texas side is managed under statewide regulations with no exceptions. For recreational anglers fishing Mexican waters, a Mexico fishing license is required for everyone in the boat. Mexico boat permits are no longer required. Mexico licenses can be purchased in Zapata at Robert's Fish N' Tackle (2425 S. Highway 83, 956-765-1442) or from Falcon Lake Tackle (2195 S. Highway 83, 956-765-4866).

Contact: Zapata County Chamber of Commerce, (800) 292-5253; Falcon Lake State Park, (956) 848-5327; Texas Parks and Wildlife District Office, (210) 348-6355

Big water and fantastic sunrises await anglers who come to fish for largemouth bass on Falcon Reservoir.

Big Bend Region

57 Amistad Reservoir

Description of area: Amistad is another border lake shared with Mexico, located approximately 12 miles north and west of Del Rio. Surface area of this sprawling rocky reservoir is 65,000 acres. The main tributaries are the Rio Grande and Devil's River. Maximum depth is 217 feet and the water clarity is usually clear. In dry years fluctuation levels can be 25 feet or more. Average is 5 to 10 feet. The lake is used for water supply and irrigation by Texan and Mexican communities. Primary fish habitat is rock structure. These include rocky points, islands, humps, steep cliffs, ledges, creek channels, and boulder piles. There are areas of aquatic vegetation in coves and on main lake points. Brushy flats also provide some cover for gamefish. The International Boundary and Water Commission is the controlling authority.

Major species: Largemouth bass, smallmouth bass, Guadalupe bass, white bass, striped bass, catfish

Rating of fishery: Largemouth bass is excellent. Catfish and white and striped bass are good. Smallmouth and Guadalupe bass are fair.

The fishing: Amistad may be the best lake in Texas currently to catch numbers of very large bass. Adequate inflow of precipitation the last several years has kept habitat in top shape, and the good forage base and long growing season have resulted in high numbers of large fish available to anglers. The sheer size of the reservoir and the irregular shoreline provide many excellent places to fish for bass. Bass begin to move to spawning areas in the backs of coves as early as December, providing excellent shallow-water fishing in winter. Spinner baits, top waters, plastic creature baits, and jigs are excellent lure choices to catch them.

In the warm months bluegill-pattern crankbaits and jigs in black and blue colors fished on main lake points and in the submerged grass beds are proven producers of good fish. California Creek, San Pedro, and Turkey Creek areas are hot spots. The mouth of Devil's River is another prime location for bass. Smallmouth anglers usually do well fishing the Devil's River mouth or the Box Canyon or Cow Creek areas with drop-shot rigs fished 25 to 45 feet deep. Crawfish-colored deep-diving crankbaits fished along the rocky points and ledges are good producers too. White bass are easiest to find and catch when they run up the rivers to spawn in late winter. Small spoons, crankbaits, and jigs in shad colors will catch them. In the summer they will school on main lake points and the mouths of major coves. Small top waters, slabs, and spinners are excellent choices to entice them. Striped bass behave much as their cousins the white bass do. Favorite means of catching stripers include throwing large top waters along shorelines early in the morning and trolling large white jigs with trailers or drifting live shad or sunfish along the river channels

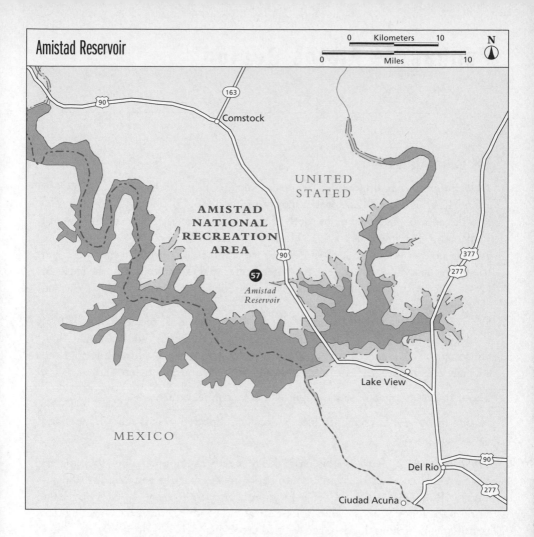

during the day. Zorro Canyon, Castille Canyon, and the flats near the dam are hot spots. Catfish are present throughout the lake and respond to live or cut bait and stink and cheese baits fished on the bottom.

Directions: From Del Rio travel west on US 90 approximately 12 miles to the Diablo East boat ramp maintained by the NPS. Daily boat launch fee.

Map: DeLorme: Texas Atlas and Gazetteer: Page 86 B3

Additional information: Ten park areas are maintained around Amistad by the National Park Service. Contact the NPS for camping and fees information. The fishery is managed under Texas state regulations. Anglers venturing into Mexican waters are required to have a Mexican fishing license for all occupants in the boat. A free map of the area is available from the NPS at Amistad.

Contact: National Park Service, (830) 775-7491; Texas Parks and Wildlife District Office, (210) 348-6355; Del Rio Chamber of Commerce, (830) 775-3551

Panhandle Plains Region

58 Lake Alan Henry

Description of area: Impounded on the Double Mountain Fork of the Brazos River, Alan Henry is a 2,900-acre water-supply reservoir for the city of Lubbock. The lake lies approximately 65 miles south of the city and just east of the community of Justiceburg. Maximum depth is 100 feet and water levels fluctuate 1 to 4 feet in an average rainfall year. Water clarity ranges from somewhat turbid in the upper end to mostly clear in the lower. Aquatic vegetation is sparse and limited to the backs of coves. The most prevalent gamefish cover is flooded brush. The lake is narrow and shorelines are rocky and steep.

Note: A consumption warning is in effect for Alan Henry. For blue catfish, flathead catfish, crappie, largemouth bass, and spotted bass, adults should limit consumption to no more than two 8-ounce meals per month. Children under 12 and women who are pregnant or nursing should not consume any fish of those species.

Major species: Largemouth bass, spotted bass, crappie, catfish

Rating of fishery: Largemouth bass is excellent. Spotted bass is fair. Crappie and catfish are good.

The fishing: Alan Henry is a big bass lake. Since it was impounded in 1993, anglers have caught and entered 25 largemouth bass into Texas Parks and Wildlife's Share-Lunker Program. Bass must weigh 13 pounds or more to be accepted. Only Lake Fork in the Piney Woods region of East Texas has produced more bass meeting that requirement. Fishing flooded, brush-lined creek channels and drop-offs are where most bass are caught in Alan Henry. The lake is deep and narrow with ledges, rock piles, and steep drop-offs providing primary main lake cover. Anglers do best in early spring during the spawning season when bass move shallow. Jigs, plastic creature baits, and crankbaits are favorite lures on Alan Henry. "Fish the brush" is the rule for anglers wanting to tangle with a double-digit-weight bass. The lake record for the species is 15 pounds and was caught March 31, 2006. Spotted bass fishing is also very good on Alan Henry. Drop-shot rigs with finesse worms and small tube jigs and crankbaits in crawfish colors are effective for catching them. Most spotted bass catches occur on the dam end of the reservoir. Crappie anglers do well on Alan Henry fishing the flooded timber in the creek channels and around the fishing pier in the Sam Wahl Recreation Area located on the north side of the lake. Spring and fall are the best months to locate them. Small minnows and jigs in white and yellow patterns are the best attractors. Rocky Creek and Gobbler Creek are hot spot areas. Catfish numbers are good and they can be caught on natural and cut bait in the coves and the river channel.

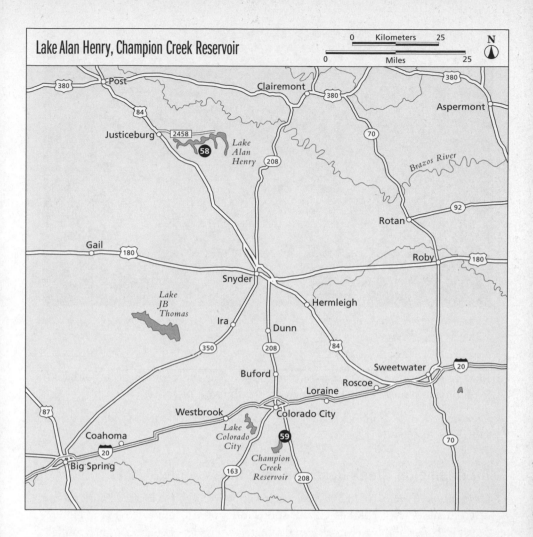

Lake Alan Henry, Champion Creek Reservoir

Directions: From the city of Post, travel south on US 84 approximately 15 miles to FM 2458. Turn east and follow it for 2.5 miles. Continue east on FM 3519 for 3 miles to the lake entrance at Sam Wahl Recreation Area.

Map: DeLorme: Texas Atlas and Gazetteer: Page 42 D3

Additional information: The only access to the lake is through the Sam Wahl Recreation Area, operated by the city of Lubbock. There is a 4-lane boat ramp and parking for about 100 vehicles. A boat ramp fee is charged. There are no improved campsites for RVs in the recreation area. Primitive sites for self-contained camping are available. Private camping sites with hookups are available at Grubbs Bait and Tackle, located just before the recreation area entrance. The fishery is managed under statewide regulations with special regulations for bass. There is no minimum length limit for largemouth bass. Five largemouth bass can be kept daily but no more than 2 can be less than 18 inches in length. The minimum length for

Steep, rocky shorelines and quality largemouth bass are predominant in Lake Alan Henry near Lubbock.

smallmouth and spotted bass is 18 inches. Daily bag limit for all species of bass is 5, of which no more than 3 can be either smallmouth or spotted bass.

Contact: City of Lubbock, (806) 629-4259; Texas Parks and Wildlife District Office, (806) 655-4341

59 Champion Creek Reservoir (see map on page 121)

Description of area: This 1,500-acre water-supply reservoir is located 7 miles south of Colorado City on the north and south forks of Champion Creek. Maximum depth is 28 feet and water levels can fluctuate widely depending on annual rainfall. Water clarity is usually turbid after runoff but remains mostly clear year-round. Gamefish habitat consists of brushy flats, rock ledges, humps, drop-offs, old farm pond dams, and riprap areas. The community of Colorado City is the controlling entity.

   Note: At press time all public ramps are closed due to low water levels. Small boats can be launched from the shore. Call for information before going.

Major species: White bass, largemouth bass, crappie, channel catfish

Rating of fishery: White bass is excellent. Largemouth bass, crappie, and catfish are good.

The fishing: Largemouth bass fishing is best during the spring and fall. When bass go shallow in late winter to early spring, fishing for them with spinner baits, top waters, and soft-plastic creature lures will produce strikes. In the summer they will suspend along ledges, humps, and drop-offs. Deep-diving crankbaits and jigs are effective tools for reaching them. In the fall fish the main lake points and rocky ledges with crayfish-colored crankbaits or shad-imitating top waters early in the day. The lake record for bass is over 11 pounds. Fishing for crappie around flooded brush in the spring with minnows and small jigs is usually productive. After spawning they move to underwater humps, rocky points, and ledges in deeper water. White bass will run up the creeks, where they are easily fooled by small shad-colored lures, in late winter. In the summer and fall, they will suspend on main lake points, underwater humps, and along the dam. Top waters early in the morning will take surface-feeding fish, and fishing live shad or minnows over deep-water structure will produce fish during the day. Trolling crankbaits and jigs is also a popular method for locating them in the summer and fall. Channel catfish are abundant. Good places to find them are the brushy flats, the creek channels, and underwater humps. Natural and prepared baits will produce good numbers of fish.

Directions: From Colorado City travel south on SH 208 for 7 miles. Look for the Fisher Park road sign and exit west. Follow road for 2 miles to park entrance. A fee is required to enter the park.

Map: DeLorme: Texas Atlas and Gazetteer: Page 42 K5

Additional information: Call the park office to determine if park is open and if water levels are adequate to launch a boat as this lake can fluctuate widely. The fishery is managed under statewide regulations with no exceptions. Colorado City offers angler- and camper-related services.

Contact: Fisher Park lake office, (325) 728-5331; Colorado City Chamber of Commerce, (325) 728-3403; Texas Parks and Wildlife District Office, (325) 651-5556

60 Lake Nasworthy (see map on page 124)

Description of area: Located on the middle Concho River just southwest of the city of San Angelo, Nasworthy is a 1,380-acre reservoir constructed for municipal and industrial water supply. Maximum depth is 29 feet and water clarity remains slightly stained. This is a constant-level reservoir maintained with discharges from nearby Twin Buttes Reservoir. The lake has abundant submerged native aquatic vegetation providing excellent largemouth bass habitat. Artificial brush piles have been added to the reservoir to improve habitat conditions for bass, crappie, and other gamefish species.

Major species: Largemouth bass, crappie, catfish, white and hybrid striped bass

Rating of fishery: Largemouth bass fishing is excellent. Crappie, catfish, and white and hybrid striped bass are good.

The fishing: Fishing the vegetated shorelines accounts for most bass caught from Nasworthy. Top waters, spinner baits, and buzz baits are all good choices to entice them early in the day. The lake record is 12.71 pounds. Fishing the edges of vegetation with Wacky worms and other unweighted soft-plastic lures is a proven tactic during the day. Spring is the best time to hook up with the large bass this lake contains. Crappie

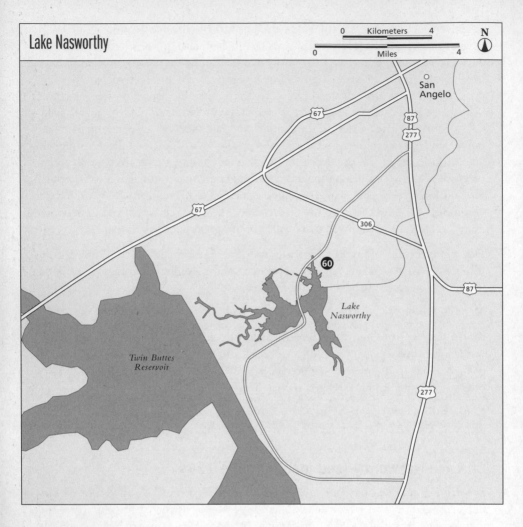

fishermen do well fishing the various man-made structures located around the shoreline using small minnows and jigs. The FM 584 Bridge pilings are a favorite location to find them after they spawn in the spring. Brush piles are also favored places to find good numbers of crappie. White bass and hybrid striped bass move up the lake in the spring into the mouths of tributaries and can be caught on live minnows and small shad-imitating lures. During the summer look for them on main lake points, creek channels, and the dam area. Trolling jigs and crankbaits or drifting live shad are favorite tactics to catch them. Catfish are prolific and respond to natural, cut, and live bait fished around structure along the shoreline, on main lake points, in creek channels, and around brush piles.

Directions: From San Angelo take FM 584, also known as Knickerbocker Road, south. Cross the FM 584 Bridge to Knickerbocker Park, located on the south shore of Nasworthy. This is a free ramp operated by the city of San Angelo.

Map: DeLorme: Texas Atlas and Gazetteer: Page 55 H7

Additional information: Most of the access parks and boat launch ramps are operated by the city of San Angelo. Call for details. There are some private areas available around the lake. Call the San Angelo Chamber of Commerce for information on lodging and other angler-related services available in the area. The lake was stocked for several years with red drum. That practice has been discontinued but there remains a possibility of catching some of the remnant population. There is no restriction on size or number of redfish caught from Nasworthy. All other fish are subject to statewide regulations.

Contact: City of San Angelo, (325) 657-4206; Texas Parks and Wildlife District Office, (325) 651-5556; San Angelo Chamber of Commerce, (325) 655-4136

61 Lake O. H. Ivie (see map on page 126)

Description of area: O. H. Ivie is a 19,000-acre impoundment on the Colorado and Concho Rivers about 55 miles east of the city of San Angelo. Maximum depth is 119 feet. Water clarity is usually clear in the main lake and the Concho River arm. The Colorado arm is usually somewhat stained. The Colorado River Municipal Water Authority is the controlling agency. Native and exotic vegetation is present in most areas of the reservoir. The lake basin experienced minimal clearing during reservoir construction. As a result, there are large areas of flooded, brushy cover in Ivie. Main lake structure consists of rocky ledges, humps, islands, boulder piles, and creek and river channels.

Major species: Largemouth bass, smallmouth bass, catfish, crappie, white bass

Rating of fishery: Catfish and white bass are excellent. Largemouth bass, smallmouth bass, and crappie are good.

The fishing: Largemouth bass fishing is very good in O. H. Ivie. Anglers have entered 23 bass in the ShareLunker Program that weighed over 13 pounds. Three of them were caught by a husband and wife team. The lake is subject to droughty conditions, as are all reservoirs in this region, that impact available habitat for bass and other gamefish species. Targeting shallow, vegetated areas in the spring is an excellent tactic for luring bass into striking. Top waters, spinner baits, large plastic worms on Carolina rigs, and crankbaits are favorite lures on Ivie in the spring. During the warm months fish the edges of creek channels with brushy cover and rocky points with jigs, spoons, and deep-diving crankbaits. Lake Record Ridge and Deadman's Bluff are hot spots. Smallmouth bass fishing is best on the southern end of the lake near the dam. Small crankbaits, tube jigs, and drop-shot rigs fished around South Island, Observation Point, and the Concho River channel will produce fish. White bass can usually be found along the main river channels between North Island and the dam. Trolling small crankbaits and jigs is a popular tactic for catching them. Drifting live shad along the river channels and adjacent flats will also take fish. In late winter they run up the rivers to spawn and will fall prey to small crankbaits,

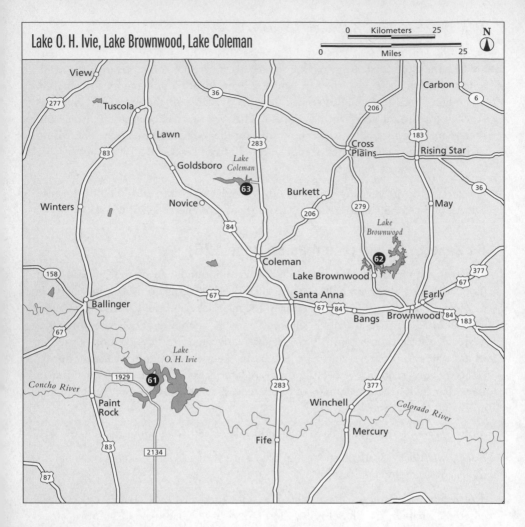

Lake O. H. Ivie, Lake Brownwood, Lake Coleman

spoons, and jigs in shad colors. Crappie anglers do well fishing the timbered creek channels, rocky drop-offs, and the main river channels with small minnows and jigs. Catfishing is good in the Concho River, Spring Creek, and Grape Creek areas on natural and prepared cheese baits.

Directions: From Ballinger drive south on US 83 approximately 15 miles to RR 1929. Turn east and follow the road for approximately 14 miles to Concho Recreation Area turnoff. There is a small per-vehicle entrance fee.

Map: DeLorme: Texas Atlas and Gazetteer: Page 55 F11

Additional information: Three areas around O. H. Ivie are operated by the Colorado River Municipal Water District. Services vary, but all provide camping and boat-launching facilities. Call for details. The fishery is managed under statewide regulations with these exceptions: Smallmouth bass must be a minimum of 18 inches in length to be retained. There is no minimum length for largemouth bass but only 2 bass less than 18 inches can be kept. The daily bag limit for all species of black bass is 5 per day, of which only 3 can be smallmouth bass.

Contact: Concho Recreation Area, (325) 357-4466; Ballinger Chamber of Commerce, (325) 365-5611; Texas Parks and Wildlife District Office, (325) 651-5556

62 Lake Brownwood (see map on page 126)

Description of area: Brownwood is a 6,500-acre reservoir impounded on Pecan Bayou and Jim Ned Creek approximately 10 miles north of the city of Brownwood. Maximum depth is 95 feet at full capacity. Water clarity is usually clear to slightly stained and levels fluctuate moderately in normal rainfall years. Brown County Water Control and Irrigation District 1 is the controlling agency. Shoreline brush, reeds, and bulrush are the main sources of vegetated habitat. Standing timber is available in the creek arms. The lake has a very irregular shoreline with many small inlets, coves, and points providing a large area of fish-attracting structure. The main lake offers boat docks, rocky ledges, humps, and flooded creek channels that provide additional habitat.

Major species: Largemouth bass, catfish, crappie, white and hybrid striped bass

Rating of fishery: White and hybrid striped bass are excellent. Largemouth bass and catfish are good. Crappie is fair.

The fishing: Largemouth anglers concentrate their efforts in the spring, fall, and winter on Brownwood. When bass move shallow to spawn, fishing top-water lures, spinner baits, and plastic worms around flooded vegetation will get their attention. After spawning, bass will retreat to the creek channels, rocky points, boathouses, and lake points in deeper water. Jigs, crankbaits, and Carolina-rigged plastic creature baits will tempt them. White bass and hybrid striped bass will move to the mouth of tributaries in late winter. Shad-imitating crankbaits, jigs, and spoons are excellent lure choices to catch them. During the summer and fall, these open water fish will haunt the creek channels and main lake points feeding on schools of shad. Drifting live shad over the suspended schools or vertically jigging a slab or spoon through them will get their attention. Early mornings these fish will push shad to the surface, creating exciting top-water fishing opportunities. Look for fish-eating birds diving to the surface to pinpoint this activity. Small top waters, lipless crankbaits, and swim baits will get hammered. Catfish can be caught in the creek channels and adjacent brushy flats on cut bait, cheese, and stink baits. Crappie fishing can be good up the tributaries in early spring and around the boat docks. Night fishing around lighted boat docks is also a popular means of catching them. Jigs and swim baits are usually the most productive lures.

Directions: From Brownwood travel north on SH 279 approximately 3 miles and turn right on FM 2632. Follow for approximately 4 miles to the dam. The launch ramp is located on the north side of the dam. There is no fee for launching.

Map: DeLorme: Texas Atlas and Gazetteer: Page 56 D3

Additional information: Several angler-related services, including marinas and tackle shops, are available around the lake. Four areas offer launch ramps and Brownwood State Park has overnight camping facilities, cabins, a fishing pier, and other amenities. Call for details. Mountain View Lodge has camping sites and a launch ramp for a fee. Several private fishing piers for a fee are also available on Brownwood. The fishery is managed under statewide regulations with no exceptions.

Contact: Lake Brownwood State Park, (325) 784-5223; Brownwood Chamber of Commerce, (325) 646-9535; Texas Parks and Wildlife District Office, (325) 692-0921

63 Lake Coleman (see map on page 126)

Description of area: Coleman is a 2,000-acre water-supply reservoir located on Jim Ned and Rough Creek approximately 13 miles north of the city of Coleman. Maximum depth is 48 feet and water levels fluctuate 2 to 5 feet in years of average rainfall. Water clarity is usually clear to slightly stained. The city of Coleman is the controlling agency. As with most reservoirs in this region, the shoreline is rocky with some aquatic vegetation in coves and creeks. Brushy species including water willow provide areas of additional cover. The upper end of the reservoir has significant amounts of standing timber that also provide excellent bass and crappie habitat. Main lake structure and cover consist of rock ledges, main lake points, boat docks, and brush.

Major species: Largemouth bass, hybrid striped bass, catfish, crappie

Rating of fishery: Largemouth bass, hybrid striped bass, catfish, and crappie are good to excellent.

The fishing: Coleman has been heavily stocked with hybrid striped bass since 2004 and a new lake record for the species was caught in 2006. That fish weighed almost 13 pounds. Favorite methods to catch them include drifting live shad along the creek channels, bouncing slabs off the bottom, and fishing top water when they herd shad to the surface. Trolling crankbaits and jigs work well too. Target main lake points and near the dam. Largemouth bass fishing is very good in late winter when bass move to shallow areas to build nests. Top-water lures, spinner baits, jigs, and plastic worms are proven producers. The lake record for this species is 12.9 pounds. During the summer weightless plastic worms and jerk baits fished along the edges of creek channels with timber and deep-water boat docks will take good bass. Crappie will be found along the creek banks in early spring and in the timbered creek channels and around boat docks after they spawn. Small jigs, swim baits, and minnows will produce good catches. The upper end of the lake along the creek channels is good for catching catfish on live bait, cut bait, and stink bait. This lake has a good population of flathead catfish. Fishing the timber in the upper end just off the channels with live shad or sunfish is a good way to catch them.

Directions: From Coleman travel north on US 283 for approximately 12 miles. Turn west on FM 1274 and follow for 3 miles to the boat ramp. Launching is free.

Map: DeLorme: Texas Atlas and Gazetteer: Page 55 B12

Additional information: Press Morris Park has angler- and camping-related services including improved and primitive campsites. A marina and bait shop is open seasonally. Call the city of Coleman for details. The fishery is managed under statewide regulations with no exceptions. Other services are available in Coleman.

Contact: City of Coleman, (325) 625-4116; Coleman County Chamber of Commerce, (325) 625-2163; Texas Parks and Wildlife District Office, (325) 692-0921

64 Hubbard Creek Reservoir (see map on page 130)

Description of area: Hubbard Creek is a 15,000-acre water-supply reservoir located 5 miles west of Breckenridge on Hubbard and Sandy Creek. Maximum depth is 60 feet at conservation pool. Water fluctuations are generally moderate, from 2 to 5 feet in normal runoff years. Water clarity is usually clear to slightly stained. The West Texas Municipal Water District is the controlling agency. The irregular shoreline offers many locations to fish for cover-oriented species such as largemouth bass and crappie. There are generous areas of flooded standing timber, shoreline brush, rocky points, submerged and emerged aquatic vegetation in tributaries, and numerous brush piles along the creek channels.

Major species: Largemouth bass, crappie, catfish, white bass

Rating of fishery: Crappie is excellent. Largemouth bass, catfish, and white bass are good.

The fishing: Hubbard is known for its excellent crappie fishing. Look for them to spawn along the brushy shorelines and up the tributaries in early spring. Dabbling small jigs or minnows around flooded brush is a fun and productive method to catch a mess of them. After spawning they will move to standing timber in the creeks and to brush piles in 10 to 15 feet of water. An excellent area to find them after their reproductive rites are complete is the US 180 Bridge. Vertical jigging or minnow fishing are the best methods to catch them. White bass will run up the tributaries in late winter and are easy to catch on small spoons, jigs, and crankbaits fished in the creek channels and pools on outside bends of the creeks. During the summer and fall, look for them on deep-water structure and main lake points. Jigging slabs over suspended fish or live shad drifted along the ends of points, humps, islands, or the creek channels should take good numbers of fish. They can also be caught on top-water lures when they are pushing schools of shad to the surface and feeding on them. Look for diving, fish-eating birds to help locate this behavior on the main lake. Water clarity on this reservoir makes fishing top-water lures for largemouth bass a win-win proposition. Look for bass around flooded brush, the edges of vegetation along creek channels, and point drop-offs. Spinner baits, jerk baits, and crankbaits are all good lure choices. In the summer top-water action is good early in the day. Later, switch to bottom-bouncing plastic worm rigs, jigs, drop-shot rigs, and deep-diving crankbaits fished along main lake points and creek channels with standing timber and around brush piles. Catfish can be caught on

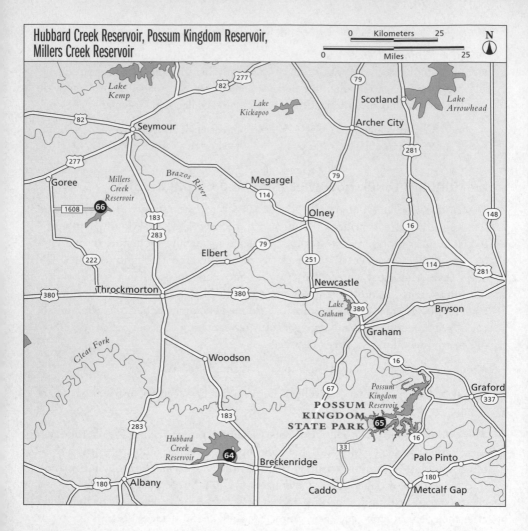

drift rigs using live or cut bait along main lake points, brush piles, and around bridge pilings and creek channels in the upper end of the reservoir.

Directions: From Breckenridge travel west on US 180 approximately 6 miles. Cross the dam and continue to the turnoff for Peeler Park. Turn north and follow to boat ramp. No fee required for launching.

Map: DeLorme: Texas Atlas and Gazetteer: Page 44 F2

Additional information: Several private campgrounds and marinas are located around Hubbard Creek. Other angler-related services including motels and tackle shops can be found on US 180 and in Breckenridge. Four areas offer public boat launching with no fee. Call the Breckenridge Chamber of Commerce for details on these services. The fishery is managed under statewide regulations with no exceptions.

Contact: Peeler Park, (325) 673-8254; Breckenridge Chamber of Commerce, (254) 559-2301; Texas Parks and Wildlife District Office, (325) 692-0921

65 Possum Kingdom Reservoir (see map on page 130)

Description of area: Possum Kingdom is considered one of the most scenic impoundments in Texas. The 17,600-acre reservoir is located on the Brazos River approximately 75 miles west of Fort Worth. Maximum depth is 145 feet and water fluctuations vary from 5 to 20 feet annually depending on runoff. The water remains mostly clear in this rocky, sinuous impoundment. Shoreline areas in the main lake are steep and rocky, with many small inlets and points. Boat docks provide additional habitat. The upper end of the lake has emerged shoreline vegetation in the inlets, and standing timber and fallen trees also provide gamefish habitat. Submerged aquatic vegetation can be found in the backs of coves throughout the lake. The Brazos River Authority is the controlling agency.

Major species: White bass, striped bass, largemouth bass, crappie, catfish

Rating of fishery: White bass is excellent; catfish is good. Largemouth bass, crappie, and striped bass are fair.

The fishing: Possum Kingdom's fishery was severely impacted by golden alga blooms in 2001 and 2003. Largemouth bass and striped bass were the two gamefish species most impacted by the toxic alga. The lake has since been restocked with those species and has made an excellent recovery. Numbers of fish available are now considered good to excellent. Sizes of striped bass and largemouth bass are rapidly improving. Largemouth bass anglers do well fishing the backs of coves in the spring with top waters, jerk baits, and plastic creature baits and crankbaits. After spawning, bass will relocate to creek channels, rocky ledges and points, and boat docks. The Stump Patch and Hell's Gate are hot spots. Drop-shot rigs, deep-diving crankbaits, and jigs are excellent lures to catch their interest. Because of the very clear water, anglers do best using the smallest pound test line possible in order to fool the bass into striking. White bass are easiest to locate and catch in late winter when they move to the mouth of tributaries and up the Brazos to spawn. Small jigs, spoons, and crankbaits fished in the channels and pools will generate strikes.

During the summer and fall, the whites will move to main lake points, drop-offs, the edges of islands, and other deep-water structure. Drifting live shad or jigging a spoon vertically over suspended fish are productive techniques for enticing them. Costello Cut and Bird Island are hot spots. Striped bass behave much the same as the white bass do. Drifting live shad over deep-water structure including main tributary channels, adjacent flats, and main lake points are good tactics to find them. Trolling large crankbaits and jigs with white trailers will also take fish. Early-morning topwater action is also possible with both species. The dam area and Bee Creek are prime locations. Look for diving birds to help locate fish feeding on shad on the surface and throw swim baits, slabs, or large top-water lures in shad colors. Crappie fishing is fair on minnows and jigs around flooded timber and boat docks. Rock Creek and Carter Creek are good locations to find them. Catfish can be caught on live or cut bait in the Peanut Patch, the flats out from the state park, or at Bluff Creek.

Directions: From Breckenridge travel east on US 180 approximately 15 miles to Park Road 33. Turn north and follow to Possum Kingdom State Park.

Map: DeLorme: Texas Atlas and Gazetteer: Page 44 F6

Additional information: The Brazos River Authority (BRA) maintains 6 facilities on PK that offer camping and other angler-related services. Contact the BRA for details on each site. The state park operated by Texas Parks and Wildlife also has camping and other amenities available. The state park is closed to camping from December 1 to March 3. Day-use facilities in the park are available year-round. At least a dozen private ramps are also scattered around the lake. A boat permit for all registered boats is also required on PK. These are available from local vendors, the BRA lake office, and from ticket dispensers located at launch ramps. There is a small per-day fee. The fishery is managed under statewide regulations with the following exceptions: The minimum length limit for largemouth bass is 16 inches. Daily bag limit for all black bass species is 5 in any combination. Striped bass and hybrid striped bass must be at least 18 inches in length to retain, and the daily bag limit is 2 fish of either species.

Contact: Brazos River Authority, (940) 779-2321; Texas Parks and Wildlife District Office, (940) 766-2383; Possum Kingdom Chamber of Commerce, (888) 779-8330; Possum Kingdom State Park, (940) 549-1803

66 Millers Creek Reservoir (see map on page 130)

Description of area: Millers Creek is a 2,200-acre water-supply reservoir located approximately 27 miles northwest of Throckmorton. Maximum depth is 48 feet and water levels fluctuate 4 to 8 feet in normal rainfall years. Water clarity is usually somewhat stained. North Central Texas Municipal Water Authority is the controlling agency. Gamefish habitat consists of some native aquatic vegetation in the shallows on the upper end, rocky points, ledges, and creek channels with standing timber.

Major species: Largemouth bass, white bass, hybrid striped bass, crappie, catfish

Rating of fishery: Catfish is excellent. Largemouth bass, crappie, and white and hybrid striped bass are good.

The fishing: Both blue and channel catfish are abundant in Millers Creek. The best fishing for them is in the creek channels and adjacent flats in the upper end of the reservoir and around main lake brush piles. Cut bait, live bait, and prepared cheese or stink baits on bottom rigs will all take fish. White bass will run up the creeks to spawn when adequate flows allow access, usually in late winter. They will strike small crankbaits, spoons, and jigs fished around logjams, in deep pools, and along the edges of channels. During the summer and fall, they retreat to the dam area, main lake points, and deep-water channels. Drifting live shad or bouncing a slab off the bottom will get their attention. Trolling the deep end of the lake for hybrid stripers with deep-diving crankbaits, bucktail jigs with white trailers, or spoons are popular tactics for attracting their attention. Drifting live shad across main lake points on the dam end of the reservoir is also a productive method of catching them. Crappie anglers find fish up the creeks during their spring spawning season and around standing timber and main lake brush piles during the summer and fall. Small jigs, swim baits, and minnows are the usual lure choices.

Directions: From Throckmorton take US 380 west to SH 222. Turn north and follow for approximately 18 miles to FM 1608. Turn east and follow signs to boat ramp. No fee required to launch.

Map: DeLorme: Texas Atlas and Gazetteer: Page 44 B1

Additional information: The Texas Parks and Wildlife ramp on the west side of the lake is the only public access to Millers Creek. Amenities include a boat ramp, cleaning station, courtesy boat dock, and primitive campsites only. The fishery is managed under statewide regulations with no exceptions.

Contact: Texas Parks and Wildlife District Office, (940) 766-2383; Throckmorton Chamber of Commerce, (940) 849-3076

67 Lake Arrowhead (see map on page 134)

Description of area: Arrowhead covers 15,000 surface acres and is located on the Little Wichita River 15 miles south and east of the city of Wichita Falls. Maximum depth is 45 feet and water levels fluctuate 4 to 6 feet in an average rainfall year. Water clarity remains somewhat stained year-round. The city of Wichita Falls is the controlling entity. The lake has a very irregular shoreline with multiple small coves and inlets. A significant amount of standing timber in the upper end of the lake and in the backs of most coves provides gamefish habitat. Shorelines are rocky. Main lake points, boulder piles, and abandoned oil derricks provide additional habitat. When water levels are adequate, a significant amount of aquatic vegetation is available along shoreline areas and in the shallow ends of coves and tributaries. Riprap along the dam also provides good habitat.

Major species: Largemouth bass, crappie, white bass, catfish

Rating of fishery: Crappie, white bass, and catfish are excellent. Largemouth bass is good.

The fishing: White crappie are abundant and eagerly sought by anglers in the spring on Arrowhead. The lake record is 3 pounds. Crappies move to shallow shoreline areas in the coves, on lake points, and around boat docks, standing timber, and riprap to spawn. Small jigs, spinners, and minnows are favorite lure choices to catch them. After spawning they will relocate to boat docks in deep water, brush piles, bridge pilings, and the oil derricks in 12 to 20 feet of water. Largemouth bass fishing is good along shoreline areas with aquatic vegetation and other forms of natural cover in the spring. Top waters, plastic creature baits, spinner baits, and lipless crankbaits fished in water 2 to 5 feet deep will attract them. During the rest of the year, fishing the riprap, creek channels, brush piles, and main lake points are productive places to find them. Crankbaits, swim baits, and jerk baits will all catch fish. The dam area and Sail Boat Cove are hot spots. Fishing around brush piles and bridge pilings with jigs will also produce good fish. Catfish numbers are excellent

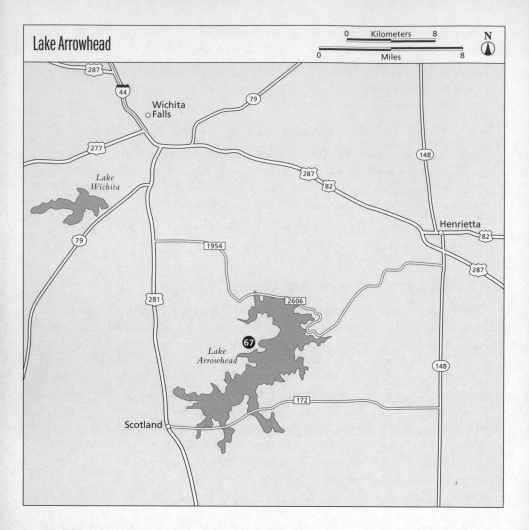

on Arrowhead. Drifting cut bait along creek channels on the upper end and along main lake points and the dam will produce good stringers.

Directions: From Wichita Falls travel south on US 281 to FM 1954. Turn east and follow for approximately 8 miles to Lake Arrowhead State Park. Entrance fee required.

Map: DeLorme: Texas Atlas and Gazetteer: Page 37 J7

Additional information: Five launch ramps are available around Arrowhead. Four are maintained by the city of Wichita Falls. There is no fee for launching at these ramps. Lake Arrowhead State Park requires an entrance fee. Improved campsites are available at the park. Call for details or reservations. The fishery is managed under statewide regulations with no exceptions.

Contact: Lake Arrowhead State Park, (940) 528-2211; Texas Parks and Wildlife District Office, (940) 766-2383; city of Wichita Falls, (940) 761-7477

68 Mackenzie Reservoir (see map on page 136)

Description of area: Mackenzie is a 900-surface-acre reservoir built on Tule Creek 10 miles northwest of Silverton. Maximum depth is 150 feet and lake levels can fluctuate as much as 10 feet annually. The water remains mostly clear year-round. This is a canyon lake and shorelines are steep and rocky. The dominant cover for gamefish are rock ledges, rubble piles, islands, and main lake points. There are some coves with flooded timber, and when the lake is full, shoreline vegetation provides good habitat. This lake is in a remote location and receives little fishing pressure. The Mackenzie Municipal Water Authority is the controlling entity.

Major species: Largemouth bass, white crappie, white and hybrid striped bass, catfish

Rating of fishery: Crappie and hybrid striped bass are excellent. Largemouth bass and blue catfish are good. Channel catfish and white bass are fair.

The fishing: Most anglers fish for largemouth bass on Mackenzie and the lake supports a good population of bass in the 2- to 5-pound range, with larger fish not uncommon. The lake record for bass is over 12 pounds. Best bass fishing is in early spring when they move to shoreline areas to spawn. Crankbaits, spinner baits, soft-plastic creature baits, and jigs worked along shoreline areas with cover will entice them. Bass will relocate to drop-offs, timbered creek channels, rocky ledges, and the ends of points after spawning. Deep-diving crankbaits, jigs, spoons, and drop-shot rigs are good lure choices to reach them. Using small-diameter line is recommended on Mackenzie in order to compensate for the clear water. Hybrid striped bass are abundant in this reservoir and the lake record is just less than 13 pounds. Drifting live shad around the islands and main lake points is a proven technique for catching them. They are also susceptible to crankbaits, slabs, and jigs fished around rocky structure close to deep water. Trolling crankbaits and jigs will also take fish. Crappie anglers do best in spring during the spawn. Fishing small minnows or jigs around flooded timber, shallow, rocky structure, and along the shoreline in the backs of coves can result in good stringers. They will move to creek channels with brush piles, along rocky ledges, and to drop-offs after spawning. Catfish can be caught on cut and prepared bait around the islands, timbered coves, and creek channels.

Directions: From Silverton travel west 4 miles on SH 86 to SH 207. Turn north and continue for 6 miles to the entrance to the lake. Turn left and continue across the dam to the boat launch. A fee is required.

Map: DeLorme: Texas Atlas and Gazetteer: Page 34 B1

Additional information: Two boat ramps are available on Mackenzie. The south ramp area has primitive campsites, a marina, and restrooms for public use. A user fee is required for both facilities. Contact the Mackenzie Municipal Water Authority for details. The fishery is managed under statewide regulations with no exceptions.

Contact: Mackenzie Marina, (806) 633-4335; Mackenzie Municipal Water Authority, (806) 633-4318; Texas Parks and Wildlife District Office, (806) 655-4341

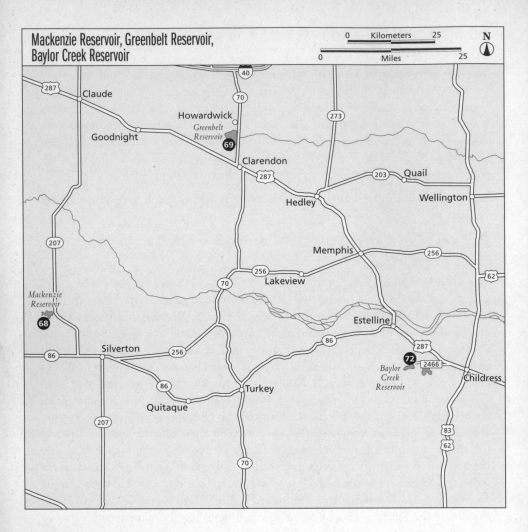

69 Greenbelt Reservoir

Description of area: Greenbelt is a water-supply reservoir of approximately 2,000 surface acres impounded on the Salt Fork of the Red River, 60 miles east of Amarillo. Maximum depth is 84 feet when full and the water remains mostly clear year-round. The Greenbelt Municipal and Industrial Water Authority in the nearby city of Clarendon is the controlling entity. Fish habitat consists of extensive areas of aquatic vegetation along shorelines, and the creek arms. Flooded timber can be found in the major creek coves. Other fish-attracting structure includes rocky ledges, drop-offs, and creek channels, riprap, and man-made structures along the shoreline.

    Note: Due to low water levels, only the Lakeside Marina ramp is open as of press time. Call the marina for updates on lake levels.

Major species: Largemouth bass, smallmouth bass, white bass, catfish, crappie, walleye

Rating of fishery: Largemouth bass is excellent. White bass, crappie, and catfish are good. Smallmouth bass and walleye are fair.

The fishing: Spring is the best time to target largemouth bass on Greenbelt. Bass move from deep water to shallow areas with cover to spawn when water temperatures reach the upper 50s F. Spinner baits, top waters, plastic creature baits, and jigs will catch them. Creek arms with aquatic vegetation or standing timber are hot spots. Later in the year, bass will move to rock ledges, creek channels, drop-offs, and other forms of deep-water cover. Drop-shot rigs, deep-diving crankbaits, and jigs are the go-to lures for enticing them. The record for this species on Greenbelt is over 12 pounds. Crappie anglers do well on jigs and minnows fishing the timbered creek channels and flooded shoreline vegetation during the spring. The riprap along the dam and rocky ledge areas will hold fish during the summer and fall. Look for white bass in the tributaries and on sandy points in the spring. Catch them on small jigs, spoons, spinners, and crankbaits. In the summer they will school and chase shad around main lake points and along the dam. Walleye have been stocked in Greenbelt since 1974 and 41,000 were placed in the lake in 2006 to supplement the existing population. Find them along rocky points and along the dam area. Use small-diameter line and small jigs, crankbaits, or minnows fished slowly on or very near the bottom. Catfish are abundant and can be caught on a wide variety of natural and prepared bait fished on the bottom in the coves and creek channels and along the dam face. Smallmouth bass are found along the rocky ledges and points and riprap areas. Small jigs, tube baits, and crankbaits in natural colors will catch them. The lake record for this species is 7 pounds.

Directions: From Clarendon travel north on SH 70 for 4 miles and turn left on County Road N. Follow to marina.

Map: DeLorme: Texas Atlas and Gazetteer: Page 70 J5

Additional information: Five ramps provide access to boaters around Greenbelt. A launch fee is required at all ramps. The lake has a special provision that all boaters must wear a life jacket at all times unless the boat is moored or beached. Several parks around the lake offer camping and other angler-related services. Contact the Lakeside Marina for details. The fishery is managed under statewide regulations with no exceptions.

Contact: Greenbelt Municipal and Industrial Water Authority, (806) 874-3650; Lakeside Marina, (806) 874-5111; Texas Parks and Wildlife District Office, (806) 655-4341

70 Lake Meredith (see map on page 138)

Description of area: Meredith is a 16,500-surface-acre reservoir impounded on the Canadian River approximately 45 miles northeast of Amarillo in the Texas Panhandle. Maximum depth is 127 feet when full, and water clarity is usually very clear in the main lake and muddy in the upper end. Water levels can fluctuate widely depending on annual runoff. The Canadian River Municipal Water Authority is the

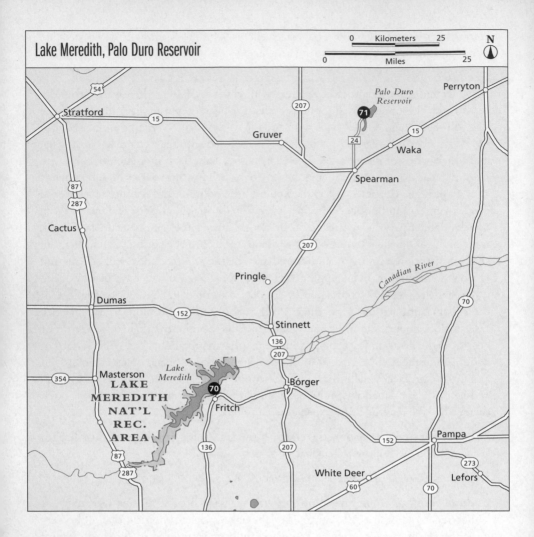

Lake Meredith, Palo Duro Reservoir

governing authority. Fish habitat consists mostly of rocky points, drop-offs, ledges, boulder piles, and steep bluffs. Some areas of shoreline and aquatic vegetation are available in the creek coves. There are also some regions of standing, flooded timber.

Note: Low water levels are plaguing Lake Meredith with an ongoing drought affecting fishing and boating access. Call the National Park Service or Texas Parks and Wildlife for the latest details.

Major species: Walleye, smallmouth bass, catfish, white bass, largemouth bass, crappie

Rating of fishery: Smallmouth bass, walleye, and white bass populations are excellent. Catfish and crappie are good. Largemouth bass is fair.

The fishing: Most anglers come to Meredith to fish for walleye and smallmouth bass. Both species prefer the rock structure readily available in Meredith. The state record walleye and state record smallmouth bass were caught from this reservoir. They weighed 7.83 and 11.88 pounds respectively. Both species reproduce naturally in this rocky impoundment and provide excellent opportunities for anglers to catch them. Spring to early summer is the best season to target both species. Most successful walleye anglers concentrate on rocky shorelines and points. The best tactic is to drift natural bait, primarily minnows or earthworms, in 10 to 20 feet of water. They can also be caught on small jigs, grubs, spinners, and crankbaits worked slowly on the bottom. During the hot season, fishing for them at night is very productive. Smallmouth anglers fish the ledges, rocky points, drop-offs, and boulder piles with soft-plastic crawfish, jigs, crankbaits, and drop-shot rigs with finesse worms to catch their favorite species. Meredith also offers excellent white bass fishing. Look for them around main lake points and humps. Jigging spoons and live bait are top producers. When they chase shad to the surface and feed on them, they are easily duped into striking small spinners, crankbaits, and top waters. Summer and fall are prime seasons to enjoy this behavior. Trolling crankbaits and spoons across points and the mouths of coves will also take these feisty gamefish. White, yellow, and chrome are the best colors to attract them. Crappie fishing is good around shoreline vegetation or brush in the spring, and flooded timber will also hold fish. Later in the year, they will retreat to drop-offs, ledges, and man-made structure along the shoreline.

The Texas Department of Health has issued a consumption advisory for walleye in Meredith. They recommend that adults should limit consumption of walleye to no more than two 8-ounce meals per month. Children should limit eating walleye from this lake to no more than two 4-ounce meals per month. The concern is elevated levels of mercury.

Directions: From Amarillo travel north on SH 136 for approximately 45 miles to Lakeview Drive in Fritch, Texas. Turn north on Lakeview and follow for about 2 miles to Harbor Bay launch ramp. Fee required.

Map: DeLorme: Texas Atlas and Gazetteer: Page 70 C1

Additional information: The National Park Service maintains 7 areas around Meredith that offer camping and boat-launch facilities. Shoreline access is limited because of the steep nature of the surrounding topography. There is a fishing pier at Spring Canyon and a fishing barge at the Meredith Marina for shore-bound anglers. Contact NPS for details on each site. Other angler-related services are available in Fritch. The fishery in Meredith is managed under statewide regulations with this exception: Smallmouth bass are subject to a 12- to 15-inch slot limit. Smallmouth bass 12 inches and smaller and 15 inches or larger can be retained. The daily bag limit is 3 fish. Walleye are managed with a 5-fish-per-day limit, but only 2 fish less than 16 inches may be retained.

Contact: National Park Service, (806) 857-3151; Lake Meredith Marina, (806) 865-3391; Texas Parks and Wildlife District Office, (806) 655-4341; Texas Department of State Health Services, (512) 834-6757

71 Palo Duro Reservoir (see map on page 138)

Description of area: This 2,400-surface-acre reservoir is located on a tributary of the North Canadian River, Palo Duro Creek, and is about 10 miles north of the city of Spearman. Maximum depth at conservation pool is 77 feet and water clarity is usually somewhat turbid. Water levels can fluctuate widely on an annual basis in this arid area. The Palo Duro River Authority is the controlling entity. Fish habitat consists of extensive areas of flooded timber and brush, native aquatic vegetation, and rocky points and ledges as well as some man-made structures, including old bridges.

Major species: Largemouth bass, crappie, catfish, walleye

Rating of fishery: Crappie and blue catfish are excellent. Walleye and channel catfish are good. Largemouth bass is only fair.

The fishing: Crappie, walleye, and catfish are the best options for anglers on this Panhandle reservoir. Populations of both are abundant and millions of walleye have been stocked in this lake since 2001. Anglers catch the greatest numbers of walleye in spring to early summer drifting live minnows or worms around rocky points, drop-offs, and ledges in 15 to 20 feet of water. Anglers can catch them on small jigs tipped with bait, small crankbaits, or jigs fished slowly on the bottom in rocky areas. Spring crappie fishing can be excellent in flooded timber and brushy areas in the upper end of the reservoir. Old bridge structures are also productive spots. Small minnows and jigs work the best. The lake also has an excellent population of channel and blue catfish. Natural, cut, and prepared baits will tempt them. The upper end of the reservoir, timbered creek channels, and the dam are good places to fish for them.

Directions: From Spearman, travel north on FM 760 approximately 8 miles to CR 24. Turn right and follow to Palo Duro River Authority Office.

Map: DeLorme: Texas Atlas and Gazetteer: Page 26 G3

Additional information: The Palo Duro River Authority operates 3 park sites with launch ramps on the lake. One is for low-water-level launching only. Call the authority for details on the sites and water level conditions. Fees are required to use the facilities. The fishery is managed under statewide regulations with no exceptions. Nearly 200,000 largemouth bass fingerlings were stocked in 2011. The city of Spearman has other angler-related services.

Contact: Palo Duro River Authority, (806) 882-4401; Spearman Chamber of Commerce, (806) 659-5555; Texas Parks and Wildlife District Office, (806) 655-4341

72 Baylor Creek Reservoir (see map on page 136)

Description of area: Baylor Creek Reservoir is a 600-acre water-supply lake on the Prairie Dog Fork of the Red River. Located 12 miles west of the city of Childress, maximum depth is 50 feet. Water fluctuations on a normal runoff year are 2 to 4 feet annually. Water clarity is usually mostly clear in the main lake and somewhat stained in the upper end. The city of Childress is the controlling entity. Gamefish habitat consists of flooded, standing timber; some aquatic vegetation in shallow areas, riprap, rocky points, and ledges; and creek channels.

Major species: Largemouth bass, crappie, catfish

Rating of fishery: Largemouth bass is excellent. Crappie and catfish are good.

The fishing: This tiny drop of water in West Texas has produced some giant bass thanks to the practice of most bass being caught and released. At least 5 bass weighing more than 13 pounds have been caught from Baylor Creek and 8-pound fish are common. The lake record weighed more than 14 pounds. Spawning season in late winter to early spring is prime time to fish Baylor. Bass will be nesting in shallow water next to cover and will fall for a variety of lures including crankbaits, spinner baits, soft-plastic creature baits, and jigs. After spawning they will move to creek channels with timber, rocky ledges, and points and riprap areas. Crankbaits, Carolina rigs, and jigs will fool them. Crappie are easiest to locate in early spring during their reproductive season. Good places to find them are in the shallow timbered areas in the upper reservoir, the backs of coves, and next to riprap areas. Small jigs, minnows, and spinners are excellent lure choices. Catfish are abundant in Baylor and fishing the timbered creeks, brush piles, and riprap areas will produce some nice fish. Baylor Creek has a good population of flathead catfish. Live or cut bait will entice them. Find them around deep-water cover and in the timbered areas.

Note: Both Baylor Creek and Childress are currently in the grip of a drought and have experienced low water levels and golden alga blooms. Fishing is poor and the lake will not be restocked until significant runoff is received.

Directions: From Childress travel west on US 287 approximately 11 miles to FM 2466. Exit and follow to boat ramp located on north side of the dam. Launch fee required.

Map: DeLorme: Texas Atlas and Gazetteer: Page 35 C8

Additional information: Baylor Creek has 2 launch ramps, both operated by the city of Childress. The south ramp has a marina, camp, picnic sites, and other amenities. Call the city of Childress for details. Childress Reservoir, also operated by the city of Childress, is a 175-acre lake located just east of Baylor Creek. It also has a good population of largemouth bass and more shoreline aquatic vegetation than Baylor. One launch ramp is available for a fee. The lake can experience low water levels. Call the marina for information. The fishery is managed under statewide regulations with no exceptions.

Contact: City of Childress, (940) 937-3684; Baylor Creek Marina, (940) 937-2102; Texas Parks and Wildlife District Office, (806) 655-4341

Appendix

Texas Parks and Wildlife Department website:
www.tpwd.state.tx.us

Online license purchase:
www.tpwd.state.tx.us/licenses/online_sales

Toll-free telephone number for general information:
(800) 792-1112

Texas Parks and Wildlife Department fisheries biologist contacts by region and district:
Region 1 Director
Bobby Farquhar
3407-B S. Chadbourne, San Angelo, TX 76903
E-mail: bobby.farquhar@pwd.state.tx.us
(325) 651-4846

District Office Supervisors
District 1A
Charles Munger
P.O. Box 835, Canyon, TX 79015
E-mail: charlie.munger@tpwd.state.tx.us
(806) 655-4341

District 1B
Spencer Dumont
5325 N. 3rd, Abilene, TX 79603
E-mail: spencer.dumont@tpwd.state.tx.us
(325) 692-0921

District 1C
Mukhtar Farooqi
3407-A S. Chadbourne, San Angelo, TX 76903
E-mail: mukhtar.farooqi@tpwd.state.tx.us
(325) 651-5556

District 1D
Randy Meyers
12861 Galm Rd. #7, San Antonio, TX 78254
E-mail: randy.myers@tpwd.state.tx.us
(210) 688-9460 or (210) 688-9516

District 1E
John Findeisen
P.O. Box 116, Mathis, TX 78368-0116
E-mail: john.findeisen@tpwd.state.tx.us
(361) 547-9712

Region 2 Director
Brian Van Zee
1601 E. Crest Dr., Waco, TX 76705
E-mail: brian.vanzee@tpwd.state.tx.us
(254) 867-7974

District Office Supervisors
District 2A
Bruce Hysmith
P.O. Box 1446, Pottsboro, TX 75076
E-mail: bruce.hysmith@tpwd.state.ts.us
(903) 786-2389

District 2B
John Tibbs
8684 LaVillage Ave., Waco, TX 76612
E-mail: john.tibbs@tpwd.state.tx.us
(254) 666-5190

District 2C
Marcos De Jesus
505 Staples Rd., San Marcos, TX 78666
E-mail: marcos.dejesus@tpwd.state
.tx.us
(512) 353-0072

District 2D
Rafe Brock
6200 Hatchery Rd., Fort Worth, TX
76114
E-mail: raphael.brock@tpwd.state.tx.us
(817) 732-0761

District 2E
Robert Mauk
409 Chester, Wichita Falls, TX 76301
E-mail: robert.mauk@tpwd.state.tx.us
(940) 766-2383

Region 3 Director
Craig Bonds
11810 FM 848, Tyler, TX 75707
E-mail: craig.bonds@tpwd.state.tx.us
(903) 566-1615

District Office Supervisors
District 3A
Tim Bister
3802 East End Blvd. S., Marshall, TX
75672
E-mail: timothy.bister@tpwd.state.tx.us
(903) 938-1007

District 3B
Kevin Storey
2122 Old Henderson Hwy., Tyler, TX
75702
E-mail: kevin.storey@tpwd.state.tx.us
(903) 593-5077

District 3C
Rick Ott
11942 FM 848, Tyler, TX 75707
E-mail: richard.ott@tpwd.state.tx.us
(903) 566-2161

District 3D
Todd Driscoll
900 CR 218, Brookeland, TX 75931
E-mail: todd.driscoll@tpwd.state.tx.us
(409) 698-9114

District 3E
Mark Webb
P.O. Box 427, Snook, TX 77878
E-mail: mark.webb@tpwd.state.tx.us
(979) 272-1430

Golden alga:
www.tpwd.state.tx.us/landwater/water/
environconcerns/hab/ga/

**Fish stocking by species and water
body:**
www.tpwd.state.tx.us/fishboat/fish/
management/stocking/

Texas Lakes & Bays Fishing Atlas:
www.fishgame.com

Index

About the Author

Barry St.Clair is an avid outdoorsman and has been a farmer, rancher, fishery technician, outdoor outreach specialist, freelance outdoor writer and columnist for *Texas Fish and Game* magazine, and outdoor columnist for the *Athens Daily Review, Corsicana Daily Sun,* and *Palestine Herald Press* in Texas. He credits his addiction to fishing to his parents, who took him on many outdoor family adventures all over the western United States.

Barry grew up on a farm in central California and graduated from California Polytechnic State University in San Luis Obispo with a bachelor of science degree in natural resource management. He and his wife, Gail, moved to Texas in 1980, and Barry has hunted and fished across the state for the past three decades.

In 1992 Barry caught the Texas state record largemouth bass, which weighed 18.18 pounds, from Lake Fork. That record still stands. Barry and Gail reside in the countryside near Athens, Texas. Barry received a master's of science degree in biological sciences from Texas A&M University Commerce in May 2012.

Want **More** Fishing?

Check out these other titles from Lyons Press:

Fly Tying with Common Household Materials

Instinctive Fly Fishing

Joan Wulff's New Fly-Casting Techniques

Lefty Kreh's Ultimate Guide to Fly Fishing

L.L. Bean Fly Fishing for Bass Handbook

Master's Fly Box

The Orvis Guide to Fly Fishing for Coastal Gamefish

The Orvis Guide to Personal Fishing Craft

The Orvis Guide to Saltwater Fly Fishing, New and Revised

Pro Tactics™: Fishing Bass Tournaments

Pro Tactics™: The Fishing Boat

Want **More** Texas?

1001 Greatest Things Ever Said About Texas
(Lyons Press)

Birds of Texas
(FalconGuides)

Camping Texas
(FalconGuides)

Fishing the Texas Gulf Coast
(Lyons Press)

Haunted Texas
(Globe Pequot Press)

Hiking Texas
(FalconGuides)

Outlaw Tales of Texas
(TwoDot)

Scenic Driving Texas
(GPP Travel)

Speaking Ill of the Dead: Jerks in Texas History
(Globe Pequot Press)

Spooky Texas
(Globe Pequot Press)

Texas Curiosities
(Globe Pequot Press)

The Texas Hill Country Cookbook
(Globe Pequot Press)

Texas: Mapping the Lone Star State through History
(Globe Pequot Press)

Texas Off the Beaten Path
(GPP Travel)